Dancing in My Tattered Pink Dress

Grief, Guts, and Glory

by

Ruth-Ann J. Thompson

Watersprings
PUBLISHING

Dancing in My Tattered Pink Dress
Published by Watersprings Publishing, a division of
Watersprings Media House, LLC.
P.O. BOX 1284
Olive Branch, MS 38654
www.waterspringsmedia.com
Contact publisher for bulk orders and permission requests.

Printed in the United States of America.

Library of Congress Control Number: 201919299

ISBN-13: 978-1-948877-39-8

Cover Photo by Keath Luke
Cover Model - Isabel Luke
Editors: Kimberly Upchurch and Dr. Valerie Lee

Table of Contents

Dedication

To anyone who has ever felt
deep and varying emotions,
laughed in the sunlight...
or dared to believe.

Thank you...

Acknowledgements

To my children, Jai, Austin and Alexandra – you are the best parts of me, and you color my world with love. I am honored to share time and space with you. I love you more than mere words can express.

To my grandchildren, Elijah, Jaidon and Shandon – Grammie simply adores you all. You paint my life with vibrancy, make my heart sing and give me sheer joy.

To those who take ACTION to secure the future of others: Lisa Dickson, Jamole Callahan, Deanna Jones, Doris Edelmann, Nikki Chinn and the entire team. Thank you for giving me a place to feel whole, a voice that feels valued and an opportunity to reach back and influence the next generation. I consider you all to be my family.

To the Two Scoops N-PAC group - Arnie Smotherman, Marlon Powell, Eddie Jones, Twyla Jones, Joyce Calamese, Karen Deberry, Todd Tyler and the entire creative team. Your acceptance of me is a gift beyond measure.

Shout Out to the #46 Gahanna Park 'N Ride Bus Riders: Lori, Ebony, Akia, Sara, Kris, Kirstie, Marcus, Frank, Denver, Chuck, Tracy ... and the rest of the crew. You make my daily commutes enjoyable.

To my photographers, Keath Luke and Jomel Aird, and my make-up artist, Marlene Makapela, for seeing my vision and bringing it to life.

To Kelli Thompson for the extras in my photo shoot and for the use of your beautiful home.

To the media team at Watersprings Media House, LLC, for turning my vision into actuality.

To my editors, Kimberly Upchurch and Dr. Valerie Lee – you've made me look great on paper.

In Memory
of my precious son, Brandon.

Foreword

I t is rare to experience a writer that elicits every single emotion from the depths and heights and widths of your soul. The carefully chosen words from Ruth-Ann Thompson's prudently designed book has pricked and piqued those involuntary reactions from me. I was not prepared for the journey and flight this book took me on. From the title of the book, to opening the first page, to ingesting the content and to closing my eyes after the very last word, my heart was challenged. Not realizing what was to happen, my tears fell at soul-searing passages, my head reeled back with the most raucous of laughter at the hilarious descriptions of differing scenes, I sat and meditated - went into my innermost soul to ask questions of God, of the universe and of every person involved in every process of Ruth-Ann's life experience.

Now that I have satisfied this reading "experience," I feel better. My heart feels better. And I feel I am a better listener, learner and citizen of this earth. I take nothing for granted, because Ruth-Ann takes absolutely NOTHING for granted. Thank you for this amazing, courageous ride you've so generously allowed us on, Ruth-Ann. Next time, I'll fasten my seatbelt...

Beverly L. Robinson, Author
My Name is Alvonia
Assistant Vice President
Client Service Consultant
Abbot Downing

Introduction

While attending a book signing in Atlanta, Georgia, I had the pleasure of meeting and exchanging pleasantries with the late Mrs. Coretta Scott King. I couldn't keep my eyes off her as she graciously made her way through the sea of people there to support Dr. Bernice King's first published work, *Hard Questions, Heart Answers.* My childhood friend, Rev. Dr. Jai S. Haithco, shared that experience with me. Before too long, Mrs. King offered the opening remarks for her daughter's event and made a comment that has stuck with me to this very day. The widow of slain civil rights leader, Martin Luther King, Jr., insisted that one should never write a book until one has something to say. Through all the years and all the tears, I finally have something to say. Basically, I want you, the reader, to know that you can choose to thrive in whatever situation you find yourself. I encourage you to laugh instead of cry, to smile instead of frown, and to dance even if you are wearing a tattered dress. And I thank you in advance for listening.

I have two first names,
two maiden names,
three married names and been widowed twice.
I have two mothers,
two fathers,
eight sisters,
three brothers,
four husbands (well, three actually, but I count one of them twice),
four children (no matter what anyone says),
and a multitude of grandchildren, both biological and non-biological,
all of whom belong to me.
To date, I've lived in five states, moving freely between those states.

Ruth-Ann J. Thompson

This is my version,
my reality,
my portion of my life.
The life I was destined to live
I choose to live happily and joyfully...
I choose to thrive in the open field of life that God has gifted to me.
I choose to dance.

On the day that you were born your cord was not cut,
nor were you washed with water to make you clean,
nor were you rubbed with salt or wrapped in cloths.
No one looked on you with pity or had compassion enough
to do any of these things for you.
Rather, you were thrown out into the open field,
for on the day you were born you were despised.
Then I passed by and saw you kicking about in your blood,
and as you lay there in your blood I said to you, "Live!"
Then I passed by and saw you kicking about in your blood,
and as you lay there in your blood I said to you, "Live!

Ezekiel 16: 4-6 (NIV)

CHAPTER ONE

TGIF – Today God Is First*

was enjoying breakfast with a dear friend recently when he asked me where my strength comes from and how do I manage to smile and have joy after experiencing loss and pain. To me the obvious answer is my unwavering belief in God and knowing that I belong to Him. My soul is grateful that I belong to Someone greater than myself.

The first words I spoke to my four newborns on the days of their birth were, "You belong to me; I love you." It was vital to me that my next generation always understood they were wanted, they were loved, and they belonged. Years later those same words were whispered to my grandchildren as I witnessed their entrances into this world and etched their first breaths into my memory forever.

A sense of belonging. An unwavering, unshakable love. My life's work, my passion and drive are all centered around that theme – helping people understand they belong. We were all created to belong and then find our purpose where we know we belong. I've learned to embrace those I encounter, whether on an elevator, the city transit system or a public gathering. I listen to the stories, share in their experiences and enjoy their ride in this vehicle called life. It's my way of dancing through this world to the rhythm of my own drum of positivity. I seek to model inclusivity and acceptance to others.

I've seen a lot of proverbial rain in my life, rain that has caused flooding and mass destruction. I've witnessed torrential down pours that have all but wiped me out. I've seen days blend into years and with the passage of time comes inevitable change; therefore, I'm convinced all my tragedies are not behind me. That's not pessimism speaking. I don't have the personality of "Eeyore" from Winnie the Pooh. I'm not negative by nature. But life has shown me that tears will come when you least expect them. And when I am given opportunities to motivate or conduct my Healthy Grieving seminars, called Sunshine in the Shadows, I offer laughter to those who thought they'd never smile again. It is my honor to help others find their purpose and unearth priceless talents. It is rewarding to promote joy even while acknowledging sorrow.

I do this because I know what hopelessness feels like. It consumes those who feel they don't belong. It crushes the soul. So today as you read my story may you find your reason to dance. To smile. To find the happy side of life on the sunny side of the street. For me, every day is TGIF - Today God Is First. With His guidance and restoration, I am constantly reassured that I belong.

This is my story.
    This is my journey.
        This is my dance.

* Borrowed from author Os Hillman.

CHAPTER TWO

Dancing in My Tattered Pink Dress

That's what he said I was doing when he saw me. This social worker, assigned to determine the feasibility and viability of the physical plant of an orphanage in Ann Arbor, Michigan, saw me moving and grooving to the music. My dress was a faded shade of pink, he said. Tattered as well, he explained. But I was dancing nonetheless. To a tune hidden in my heart, an unsung melody of hope. Music has always inspired me to move to its syncopation. And even though I was raised to believe dancing was not something a Christian should do, I will run you over trying to get to the dance floor to do the Electric Slide. It's in my blood and that same rhythm runs through the veins of my children and my children's children.

Dancing. Alone. In a colorless and empty space where I had never heard or spoken the word "mother." Where my caretakers were paid to tend to my basic needs. Where the sun barely touched the walls in the greyish-colored rooms. Where I had no family to call my own, and no possessions to speak of. From the moment of my birth, I was a ward of the State of Michigan, residing in Ann Arbor, the city of my birth. Someone to be easily disregarded, taken advantage of, discounted. I lived among the poorest of the poor. The outcasts of society. The nobodies. Yet somehow, I was dancing. Dancing with such vigor and grace that it captured the heart of Dr. Reger Smith, Sr. Instead of making a judgment call about what my future would be, he chose instead to see me, and see who I could be.

I'm told that he couldn't get the image of that dancing little girl out of his head. He returned home to Saginaw and talked to a fellow church worker about me. Always a man of tact, he hesitantly mentioned his thoughts.

"Sister Jones?"

3

"Yes, Brother Smith?"

"Have you ever thought of having children?" he asked.

The question was felt like an exploding bomb in Versia Jones' chest. Long ago, after enduring several miscarriages, the doctors had informed her that her womb would never be able to carry a child. Her first marriage had ended because of her infertility. The pain crushed her very soul, for she longed to bear children. To be a mother was her greatest desire. To be considered barren was her deepest agony. That's why she worked with the youth of the church on Wadsworth Avenue. It enabled her to be close to children and teens. In addition to her own nieces and nephews, she became a surrogate aunt to countless others in the church.

"I am not able to have children, Brother Smith." Her eyes lowered to hide the tears.

"Have you considered adoption?"

"I have. But my husband and I are too old."

"You may be too old to be considered for an infant. But what about a child?"

"Do you think we could?"

"Not only do I think it is possible," Brother Smith offered, "but I think I saw your daughter this week! She was standing in the corner, wearing a faded and tattered pink dress, and she was dancing..."

I don't remember much about my first meeting with Mom and Daddy. I do remember taking a broken plain-colored purse to a man who gently picked me up and sat me on his knee while he fixed it. The chain on the strap was now in perfect working order and I thought this man could do anything!

I'm told that I was afraid of men, and I don't know why, although I can only imagine. But I recall that in this man's arms I felt safe.

I remember going out with them one afternoon and seeing lush green grass and a vivid blue sky. And being on a swing that allowed me to float high up into that big sky. I kept insisting that the man "swing me high!"

Squealing with delight, I was overwhelmed by the chance to play outside and breathe fresh, clean air. We stopped and ate at this long table, but we were still outside. I had a sandwich that had color on it. Yellow was the color. I still delight in the rich vibrant color and smell of French's mustard. I saw green lettuce and purple grape juice and heard the crunch of fresh potato chips. And I remember feeling happy. So happy that my eyes sprouted a waterfall.

"Why are you crying, Baby?" the kind lady had asked me.

"I'm just so happy," was my reply. Little did I realize that this kind of "happy" I was feeling was the same kind of happy that my grandfather used to speak of. I was as happy as a field lark in plowed ground. That's the kind of happy that feels contentment and satisfaction and that all is right with the world.

After their initial interviews with the adoption agency, I'm told that it took about nine months for me to come home. That's another word that I didn't know and had never heard before. Home.

My next memories are of my mother driving me home. I was in a huge car that was moving me fast. This was long before the days of seatbelts, and I rode in the front seat on my cousin, Barbara's lap. I giggled at almost everything. The water, bridges and sky intrigued me. The other cars whizzing by delighted me. The colors. How I remember the colors! They almost hurt my eyes because they were so vibrant. I don't remember any color but gray until I left that orphanage. There was probably some color in my world; I was simply unable to recognize it. But I understand my vision now, that when I'm extremely sad my eyes don't register color, only life as if I'm looking at a black and white TV. My eyesight has lost its color three other times so far in my life. And they were tragic events to me.

CHAPTER THREE

My Arbor — A Place of Rest

I learned many new words once I arrived at the small light blue ranch-styled house with white shutters and a one-car port at 131 Moton Drive. I'm using the word "small" by my standards today. Back then it looked like a sprawling mansion and I felt like I was the princess of the world. When I walked in the door, there was a living room to my right and a closet to my left. Straight back was the kitchen. Behind the closet was a short hallway, and three bedrooms and one bathroom branched off this hallway. If you continued through the kitchen, there was a back door with a small porch and green yard. Daddy kept our lawn perfectly manicured while mom worked tirelessly with her flowers and bushes. Off from the kitchen was a stairwell that led to the unfinished basement.

Our basement had a concrete floor and housed the washer, dryer, ironing board, Daddy's tools, and a deep freezer. It also had a bin where potatoes and onions were kept. When I looked at those potatoes, their eyes appeared to be blinking back at me and it terrorized me to no end. Years later my children would discover my secret fear of potato eyes and chase me throughout the house with them – me screaming bloody murder and them squealing with delight. And now, in this newfound technological age, my grandchildren just "screen shoot" the potato eyes and text them to me, knowing full well I will call them, screaming and begging them not to send me anymore "scary pictures!"

The basement became my refuge, my play area, and later my practice studio when Mom and Daddy got me a piano. I would spend many hours down there playing with friends or playing alone or concocting all types of Easy Bake Oven creations. That basement also housed Mom's fancy, "After-Five" outfits and off-season clothing, which I loved to dress up in and become the characters that would later show up in my books.

Home. It was a wonderful place to be in the summer of 1964! I was almost four years old when I learned that word. Later in life one of my greatest joys would be working with those who were ready to age out of foster care, or "care" as we call it, or those who had already aged out, the "alumni." Securing housing, educational opportunities and a place of being is so vital. We do a yearly Thanksgiving meal for our awesome youth, and it is the highlight of the season for me. Although I found a loving home, I dare not forget that "but for the grace of God, go I."

Daddy. That was another word that I had never used before. How I loved my Daddy! He wasn't extremely tall by the world's standards, but he was a giant of a man to me. Daddy's complexion was a smooth chocolate brown and he had piercing blue eyes. He insisted that his eyes were brown, and I suppose they might have been in his younger years, but the eyes I fell in love with were blue. He used to say that brown eyes were the best eyes, and one of my terms of endearment for my children and grands is, "Brown Eyes." Perhaps it's because of Daddy that I always notice the color of someone's eyes when I first meet them. Daddy's appearance was always neat and clean. No facial hair, short, slicked-back hair, shirt always tucked in, everything always matching. He walked with slightly bowed legs that seemed to afford him that rhythmic swagger that I loved to see. He commanded coolness. Yep. Daddy's "Cool Factor" was way up there! His voice was tender and loving, perhaps a baritone, and he fiercely loved me and Mom. I've heard it said that his name is synonymous with Lucifer. But I absolutely loved my Daddy's name: Lucious Detroit Jones. Daddy did not like his middle moniker at all, but I thought it just added to his Cool Factor. Once I learned his middle name, he begged me not to share that information outside of the family. It would be years before I did, well after his death, and always with tender affection. I call all my sons "Lucious" and my daughter "Lucinda Maria" or "Miss Lucy" in homage to my wonderful father. And I say his name with a whispered prayer of thanksgiving on my lips ... Lucious ... Detroit ... Jones.

Daddy was a GM man, and had worked for General Motors long enough to know every job on the line at Grey Iron Casting Foundry in Saginaw, Michigan. By the time he retired, he had given that job 48 years of his life. He worked the second shift, which meant that he wasn't home with us most evenings, but he was always there when I woke up.

Daddy's job title by the time I came home to live with them was Relief Man, which meant he would go to various workers' positions on the assembly line and relieve them so they could enjoy their lunch. However, I couldn't figure out for the life of me why Daddy would faithfully pack a lunch each day. In my opinion, he was there to "replace" them for their lunch, which in my young mind meant that he ate people's lunches for them! I was convinced that Daddy's slightly pouched belly was the result of all the lunches he had to eat at work. One day while bragging "my Daddy is better than yours" with some friends, Mom overheard me declaring, "Oh yeah? Well, my Daddy can eat everybody's lunches!" She promptly explained to me what Daddy's real job was, but in my mind, I still held on to my own belief.

We had plenty of quality time together, especially before I began attending school. Occasionally he would take me on errands with him. We would go to the main post office downtown, and he would get me those giant Tootsie Rolls that were certain cavity-makers and would take me days to eat. We would also buy plain M&Ms, which is still my favorite candy to this day. Daddy taught me how to change the oil in the car, change tires, repair a tire, keep an impeccable lawn, and sew on a button. I learned plenty of things from Mom, too, but it seemed like my time with Daddy was magic. He often had puzzles and games for me to tackle my problem-solving skills and was forever offering riddles that I needed to solve or sharing corny jokes. For example, one day he produced a stark white sheet of paper and asked me to tell him what it was. After guessing answers like, "it's just a piece of paper" or "it's an unwritten book," he told me it was a picture of a ghost in a snow storm! We both roared with laughter!

Daddy had the best sense of humor. "You either laugh or you cry; and I choose to laugh," I would often hear him say. And he had great friends; decent, honest, hard-working men who respected their women and took care of their families. He had no tolerance for a man who would not work and he believed that going into a church didn't make you a Christian any more than going into a garage would make you a car. He said, "People will know that you are a Christian when you treat them like Christ would." He would not attend church regularly until much later in my lifetime, but I often saw him reading his Bible and praying. Watching him read his Bible sparked in me a true love for God's word. Daddy was a sermon that I could see. Daily I witnessed him caring for others and seeing to the needs of those who were "less fortunate" than us. And more than anything else, Lucious Detroit Jones would never tolerate a man hitting a woman. That was not going to happen on his watch! Not ever!

Nothing made that point clearer to me than the time Mom brought home a woman and her three young children. Although I was young, I knew something was terribly wrong with that woman's face. Now I understand that she had been beaten so badly by her husband that she was almost unrecognizable. The children looked frightened and fragile and I will never forget the look of terror in the older boy's eyes. Early the next morning, Mom guided them through the back yard and into Daddy's waiting car. He had parked on 19th Street when he came home from work the night before. It wasn't long after they left that I heard a loud banging on our front door. It was the lady's husband, loudly cursing and swearing and insisting that Daddy let him in. I was in the hallway, afraid to peek around the corner at the angry man. I could hear my father calmly explaining that this man's wife was not here and that he would call the police if this man did not remove himself from our porch. The man quieted down and left promptly, and as the door shut behind him, I heard my father mumble, "What a coward! No man should ever hit a woman!"

As I grew, he would often insist that no man was to ever put his hands on me. But he also gave me further instruction: "If a man ever hits you, don't try to fight him back, for a woman is no match for a man's strength. Just know this will be your last day with that man. Let him go to sleep and quickly pack your bags." He then gave me the exact formula to use on that bully of a man. Thankfully I have never had to make that concoction, but I always knew that I would if I ever had to do so. I later found out that Mom had taken that woman and her children to Flint, some 30 miles away, and put her on a train to Chicago. Daddy had insisted on paying for all four tickets. There my aunt and uncle took them in for a few months until she could get on her feet. Years later we would see her again, healthy, happy and thriving, and ever so grateful to my parents. They didn't need to run it by a church committee or check in with the local authorities. They saw a need, worked out a plan and saved generations from the curse of domestic abuse.

I thought that my Mom was absolutely beautiful. She was not very tall, 5'4" to be exact, full-busted with silky-smooth skin. I marveled at her flawless caramel-colored skin. Her legs were hairless and her knees were so smooth that family members insisted she had never crawled. In contrast, my knees were rough and darkened by Lord only knows what. My legs had hair on them even as a child. She always smelled good, not like perfume, but like the freshness of spring. Just one sniff made me feel secure. Years later I would crawl into her bed, hours before her death, to inhale her essence again and hear her heart beat one last time. Even as I write these words, I recall and remember ...

I smile as I recall one time when we went to Chicago for the funeral of my father's brother, Uncle Tony. Upon entering the house, we suddenly heard a loud "WHIRR-WHIRRRRRRR!" It was the type of whistle that a man would offer to a good-looking woman. Looking around to find out who did that, it was soon discovered that the family Myna bird was whistling at my mother! Every time she entered the room, he'd let out a loud, dramatic "WHIRR-WHIRRRRRRR!" After two days, my dad finally walked up to the cage and declared, "Hey Man, that's my wife you're whistling at!" The bird bowed his head and quietly whispered into his feathers, "whirr-whirrrrrrr!" The room erupted with laughter. A voice was heard to comment, "Even the birds know how fine that woman is!"

My mother was very organized and neat; I never saw our home in disarray. That is, not anywhere besides my room. I struggled with having "a place for everything and everything in its place," and clearly my thoughts on where things belonged were far different from my mother's. Mom was a stay-at-home mom, but she was more industrious than the CEO of a Fortune 500 company. She was never idle or lazy by any stretch of the imagination and would constantly find ways to make our home look beautiful. One always knew what season we were in by our home's displays and she was constantly changing decorations, knick-knacks, curtains, and bedspreads. I used to think that I could tell the very month of the year by the centerpieces that garnished our tables. The smells of our home were akin to that of a fine bakery, and I cannot recall one day while growing up that we did not have desserts baking in our oven. She believed that everyone should have a good hot meal, homemade desserts and plenty of water every day. One time the church members needed to raise funds for some project. I was too young to know all the details, but Mom decided to sell sweet potato pies during the Thanksgiving and Christmas seasons. A few ladies helped, but mostly I remember Mom boiling and toiling over those delicious pies. I don't know what their goal was, but I know that the ladies far surpassed it with Mom's golden touch. Mom made selling sweet potato pies a lucrative business long before Patti LaBelle did the same thing years later for WalMart. Patti's pies are great; but my Mom's pies were superb!

Our yard remained in bloom year-round because Mom made sure to have the proper flowers and bushes. Tirelessly and effortlessly, she worked in both the yard and the house. From the first hint of spring until the bitter Michigan cold when the snow covered absolutely everything, passersby would always find something blooming at 131. There were times when people would stop to ask about some blooming flora on display, and Mom would happily share information, sometimes clipping a portion to share while offering instructions on how to start their own vine or bush. My parents happily toiled in the yard and seemed to love it, but I just didn't want to have any parts of it. I absolutely hated all things that had to do with gardening, planting, pruning and watering. But I would never, ever say that. I just went along with it all, doing everything I could to not do what was necessary to complete the task. Eventually I was assigned the task of watering the flowers or picking the strawberries because I'm sure it didn't take them long to realize that all that outdoor stuff just wasn't for me.

Mom was also a collector of all things antique. She could make anything look exquisite and her vision never ceased to amaze me. Long into her retirement years, she supplemented her income quite well by dealing in antiques. She had an eye for quality and taught me that same skill. I have some treasured pieces and know their value. I've passed that knowledge on to my children. In her later years, it was important to me that she be surrounded with the beauty that she had created her entire life. So, in the spring I'd make the four-hour drive specifically to bring her blooming flower pots and prop them up on black wrought-iron shepherd's rods – the perfect height for her to water and tend to them. Midsummer I'd visit and make sure she got to drive around and see farmland and florals and that she had plenty of fresh produce. During the holiday seasons, I'd send homemade baked goods that delighted her. And when she could no longer live on her own, the place we chose matched the feel of home. In her final days, she was surrounded by plenty of beauty, along with loving family and friends.

Hers was a unique name, just like Daddy's. Versia Ree Stephens Jones. (Ver-SEE-ya). Her sister-in-law, Aunt Ella, and one cousin, Tennie, called her "See", which was a term of endearment. Although her name was unique, I thought of it as one of the most beautiful names I had ever heard. Her nieces and nephews called her "Aunt Versie" and so did most of the youth in the church. She happily answered to it all, but I know beyond a shadow of a doubt that her favorite name to be called was "Mommie." She smiled easily and laughed heartily. But I knew to never cross her; Momma didn't play. Mostly it was her way or no way. But that didn't matter to me. I was so grateful to be home that I had positively no complaints about anything.

Growing up, I always felt dissatisfied when it came to my looks. I believed that if they had been my actual birth parents, I would have looked better, and that my hair would have been softer and more manageable. But now I know that God designed me just the way I am for His good pleasure. I am now extremely comfortable in my own skin and so very glad to be me. I suppose that's what happiness, true happiness, is all about.

CHAPTER FOUR

Relatively Easy

Daddy was number nine of eleven "Jones Boys," and all his brothers lived in other cities, except for his youngest. Uncle Lamar was absolutely the best uncle ever! He and his wife had two daughters, and we saw them often. He would drop by to check on us and every time he came by, my Daddy was clearly pleased to see him. Uncle Lamar died when I was a teenager and that was the second of three times that I ever saw my Daddy cry. Clearly the most loved, there are many in the family who named children after this uncle, including me. Austin's middle name is Lamar.

Mom had two brothers, Uncles Wilse and Elijah Stephens. Her older sister, Gertrude, died because of injuries sustained in a fire when my mom was just nine years old. Only the two of them were home at the time and Mom watched her sister burn right in front of her. I don't know how you ever truly recover from that kind of trauma. Uncle Elijah lived in Saginaw, and we saw him often as well. He had the best personality and was always helping Mom with one project or the next around the house. He and my Aunt Ella were divorced by the time I came along, but together raised six girls. Barbara, the one on whose lap I rode all the way home from the orphanage, was the oldest. In close succession came Joyce, Ruthie, Jackie (now deceased), Linda and Cathie. I used to say I was named after Ruthie, but of course that's not true. I saw those cousins often and we shared many memories. Getting together with them, even now, brings plenty of laughter and great food. We find humor in everything, but never at each other's expense. Life's simplest pleasures bring us joy and we see the best in everyone and everything.

Uncle Wilse lived in Memphis, Tennessee, where the family moved after the tragic death of Aunt Gertrude. Uncle Wilse also had six children, three sons and three daughters: Bettie, Boyce, Venelsia (whom we all call Vanessa),

Vivian (now deceased), Joseph and Jerrell. He and his wife, Aunt Bessie, whom he lovingly called "Puddin'," welcomed me with open arms on my first visit to Memphis. My cousins acted as if I had just always been there, and I loved having extended family members.

But I think the best part of Memphis was meeting my grandparents. Momma Anna and Daddy Frank were no longer living in the same household, but clearly still loved each other with all their hearts. My mom was the "baby" of the family and acted very much like it when she was around her parents. She could get anything she wanted from her father. When he saw me, the first thing I can remember him saying to my mom was that meeting me had made him "as happy as a field lark in plowed ground." I didn't know what that meant at the time, but I knew it was something great. My grandfather was full of sayings, most of which I would not understand until many years later. But by the context and the emphasis, I could pretty much figure out the meanings. I'm sure there are plenty of sayings I have forgotten, but some of the ones that I remember are included in this book, including chapter titles.

I have fond memories of my grandfather, a carpenter and farmer, who provided both housing and food for his family and countless others. There are structures built by the hands of Frank Stephens still standing in Holly Springs, Mississippi to this day. He was known to build homes for the homeless and provide food for the hungry. Daddy Frank used to say, "There's more to religion than bumping your knees against the church floor," and he, like Daddy, believed people would rather see a sermon than hear one any day. He was practical, not judgmental.

Daddy Frank's mouth always housed a toothpick, which baffled me to no end, because he did not have a tooth in his head! I would go near him and peer deeply into that cavern of his mouth searching desperately for just one tooth, but to no avail. And he didn't mind smiling either. There was no shame in him as his lips parted to reveal the pinkest and shiniest of gums flashing ever so brightly in the noonday sun.

Momma Anna was a thin, quiet woman with a ready smile and a gentle voice. Her hair was long and thick and it took her a long time to comb it through because she was "tender-headed," which means that her scalp hurt a lot whenever it was touched or her hair was tugged. I had no idea what that was like at all. My hair was red and wooly, and I looked like a human carrot when I was a little girl! It was extremely coarse, very short and simply would not grow. It took a long time to comb my hair, not because I was tender-headed, but because my hair was difficult to manage. I now absolutely love my hair, but back then I desired to have hair that was as long and beautiful as Momma Anna's.

She moved effortlessly throughout her home always baking, preparing, cleaning or straightening, sewing or reading. Ever busy, ever moving, she was a brilliant woman who had more wisdom and kindness than anyone I've ever known. At age 17, when I was asked what I wanted for my graduation present, I quickly said that I wanted to spend time alone with Momma Anna. She was that kind of grandmother. She was known for her beautiful creations and could sew any of the latest fashions without using a pattern. It has been said that her children were the best dressed in the county, all because of her seamstress and tailoring skills. She made dresses, coats, underclothing, you name it. If it fit on a body, she could make it look like it was bought from the finest designer in the land. And it didn't take her a long time to make them. She could "whip" up an outfit in no time at all. By the time I came along, Momma Anna was more prone to alterations than creations, but when my grandmother altered my clothing, it didn't even look like the same outfit! During the bell-bottom craze, she transformed my non-stylish pants into hip-hugger specials, two-toned and ready for prime time! She also replaced some buttons on my coat one time and I didn't even recognize it!

We would make plenty of trips to Memphis, Holly Springs and to Birmingham, where Daddy's closest brother, Uncle WT lived. The two of them looked just alike, except Uncle WT was a taller, thinner version of Daddy. They walked alike and their voices sounded the same to me. Uncle WT and his wife, the other Aunt Bessie, had five children, but it would take me years to learn exactly who their sons, Jimmy and Tommy were, as they lived in other cities. Initially I met my cousins, Gloria, Carol (now deceased) and Marian and their children.

Mom was 37 and Daddy was 46 when I was born - which made them 41 and 50 by the time I came home - so all my first cousins were a lot older than me. In fact, I have two nieces and a nephew who are older. Kevin, Renae' and LaVerne were the children of Daddy's daughter, Delores (Dee) and her husband James. James Bond. I always loved the fact that he shared the same name as the fictional character! They also lived in Saginaw and we spent lots of time together. Delores was cold and aloof and I always sensed that she did not like too many people. But James? He was the dearest man! And my nieces and nephew are simply amazing. James was a man who loved to fish, hunt, ski, swim and do all things in the out of doors. We would have huge cookouts at many of the parks around Saginaw, but I remembered spending the most time at Ojibway Island Park. Everyone brought tons of food, and we would play in the water, ride the boats and ski or just hang out with each other. Our summers, holidays, and birthdays were mostly spent with James and Dee and their children.

Uncle Elijah worked at the Michigan Sugar Company in Carrollton, Michigan. We called it the sugar beet factory. In the late 1800s, after the loggers had cleared all the pine forests in the area, this land was virtually unusable. There was nothing but tree stumps left behind and the local leaders wondered what to do. The area needed jobs. Then a skilled potato grower - how fitting that his name was Lucius Lyon - decided to try to use his talents to grow sugar beets. It would take agriculture, business and a lot of hard work to turn those trees into beets, but the process brought the stump lands back into productivity. Familiar brands like Pioneer and Big Chief were the result of my uncle's hard work.

Mom, who was always looking for something unique to decorate, would call on her brother to help with this task. I knew that whenever Mom called Uncle Elijah, we were off on an adventure to the sugar beet factory. Out in those vast, never-ending, muddy fields were treasures beyond my wildest dreams. Off we'd go, just the three of us, trudging through what felt like miles and miles of vast open dirt. I hated those excursions worse than I hated yard work, primarily because I never knew what in the world we were looking for. But I knew better than to say that I disliked the task at hand. I just shuffled along with my head hanging down and every now and then Uncle Elijah would pick me up to keep me from getting too far behind them.

I later realized that sometimes Mom didn't know what she was looking for either, but she would know it when she saw it.

She found rocks that looked like potatoes to me. Pieces of wood that resembled clumps of dirt. Old metal scraps that had more rust than color on them. Old pots. Tin cans. If you could see the expression on my face as I am writing these words! Ugh! I usually left the fields with at least two bruises, a few cuts and plenty of scrapes, and I was convinced that the worst case of bubonic plague ever to hit the earth was nestled in those crevices where the sugar beets grew. I tried to cough my way, sneeze my way, limp my way, crawl my way out of going to the fields of the sugar beet factory, but to no avail.

Uncle Elijah never seemed to mind being there with Mom. It was as if he was on an awesome adventure and he was a kid again. The two of them, less than two years apart in age, would talk of the days in Holly Springs, Mississippi and the memories that siblings share. My uncle sensed my disdain for these treks, and sought to get my mind off the task at hand. He would begin a walk down memory lane at just the right time, and I'd laugh so hard I'd forget I was in the middle of absolutely nowhere. He was tall and extremely thin, and at times I wondered if the wind would just carry him away to parts unknown. But he was strong as an ox and seemed to never tire as we marched farther and farther away from the car. He was a pleasant man, given to the drink and the smoke, and loved his girls with a fierceness that matched my own father's love. I can't remember Uncle Elijah and I ever having a real conversation, but I felt like I talked to him all the time because I was there for his conversations with Mom. Now that I think about it, I never really talked with Mom's other brother, either, but somehow felt very close to them both.

After we had been there for an eternity and a half, we would head out to the rummage sales. Today we use the words Garage Sale or eBay, but back then, if you wanted gently used clothing and housewares, you had to drive from place to place and dig through other people's junk. I liked the rummage sales better than the sugar beet factory, but not by much. I remember going to one place where they had underwear for sale – 12 pair for a quarter. I just refused to wear someone else's panties! Of course, knowing that I used to live in an orphanage, Lord only knows what I wore, ate and had to touch while there.

The thing about those rummage sales was that we didn't need Uncle Elijah to go with us, so I was subjected to those horrible adventures on any given day. Mom knew the right locations to go to and usually came back with some great things at such reasonable prices, but I just never got the hang of pawing through a table full of junk to try to find something great. I would feign hunger or tummy aches, and I should have stopped that foolishness because Mom wasn't having it. She was going to find a bargain if it killed her. I was convinced that it was going to kill me.

And that reminds me of shopping, another pastime I have never learned to love. Plenty of my friends know that I go to the store to get exactly what I think I need. I don't try it on, then go to twenty other stores only to discover that I really like the first item I tried on. And I do not tolerate the shopping sprees of others. Mom cured me of that long ago.

It would take years for me to realize what an innovative and frugal woman Mom really was. Those rocks, wood clumps and metal scraps were brought home and skillfully cleaned, rubbed and polished until they took on the form of something that could be found in an expensive and exclusive art gallery. A little soap, paint and glue, along with a determination and vision like I can never describe on paper, turned those hideous forms into treasures beyond my wildest expectations. Some were restored back to their former glory, while others were repurposed and put on display in the most prominent of places. Naturally, Mom knew what she was looking at; I was just clueless.

Mom approached people much like she approached garage sales. Everyone had a purpose and value. I can remember her visiting the elderly frequently. Those jaunts taught me many things. I learned that you simply cannot discount someone based how they look when you happen their way. I learned that the elderly weren't born with gnarled fingers and hunched backs, but rather life and time had brought them to that point. When we would visit them, Mom took delightful dishes and tasty desserts. While she talked with and helped them, I marveled at the portraits of their earlier years. Many had been stunning or extremely handsome, yet I could barely find traces of that in them. All possessed a wisdom and grace that mesmerized me, and I found they could add insight into my petty troubles and seemingly mountainous problems. I learned that when you want something, go after it no matter what anyone says. Everyone doesn't have to share your vision; in fact, they may never understand why you want what you want or do what you do. No matter how much others cough, crawl, pretend they are sick and are ready to move on to something else, continue to move forward in your own space and keep your focus sharp. Your vision will materialize into a thing of beauty.

I learned that sometimes you need a little help to get what you need, and it may be from someone different than you'd hoped it would be. With Daddy at work in the afternoons, Mom needed Uncle Elijah's strength to carry these castoffs back to our car. One find especially intrigued me. It was a piece of driftwood that had somehow broken off from the tree and floated along the river and landed in the field with the sugar beets and the tree stumps. This piece of wood actually frightened me. The material of the tree looked like a loofa sponge and was full of larger holes that seemed to stare right at me, much like those potato eyes, as I recall. Me and my vivid imagination! It was heavy and awkward; much heavier than Mom or me or me and Mom together could carry. But with Uncle Elijah there, Mom got that driftwood back to the car, and best of all, I didn't have to touch it. Mom didn't do much to that stray unattached piece of wood. She cleaned it, let it dry in the sun and then put some type of sealant on it. It would stand guard at our front door for years and years to come. That taught me that sometimes we must accept people the way they are. It's not our job to change them, just to let them know they belong. Over time, I came to love that scary-looking, odd-shaped piece of wood. And in my lifetime, I have brought into my circle those who were considered outcasts and driftwood. They have made profound differences in my life and I will be forever grateful for the lessons I learned at the sugar beet factory.

There was an older woman in our church who sought to spark the entrepreneurial spirit inside of us kids. Every May she would make two types of carnation lapel boutonnieres – red and white. Anyone who wanted to earn some extra money would connect with Sister Ola Flint to sell her flowers for a quarter each and could keep a nickel for themselves. There were quite a few who were willing to sell those flowers to earn some extra cash. I was told that they would use the money to purchase their own mother a gift for Mother's Day. They sold those flowers throughout the entire city. Patrons were to purchase a red flower if their mother was still alive; or a white flower if she was no longer living.

Somehow, by the time I was almost ready for school, Mom decided that I was now old enough to join the ranks of the working children and sell Mother's Day flowers. I wasn't very good at that venture and by the end of the third day I hadn't earned a full dollar. I had sold only three flowers, and two were to my own mother! Somehow Uncle Elijah learned of my predicament and told my mother to bring me, Cathie, his youngest daughter, and a few others out to Crooked Creek Bowling Alley, a favorite hang-out spot on the far west side of town. Mom gathered up the group of us girls and off we went to sell our flowers. Uncle Elijah met us there and began to help us by calling out to his drinking buddies, "Who loves your mother? If you love your mother, buy these flowers from my girls!" With his help, we sold all our flowers. I had more money than I had seen in my short lifetime. But I knew who had done all the work, and I knew that peddling flowers was not my gift. In May of 2010 it dawned on me that I would now have to purchase a white flower, should that option be given to me again, for my mother was no longer living. The reality of that fact caused me to cry all day long.

Uncle Elijah was a constant visitor to our home. Sometimes we'd see him regularly and sometimes it would be months before we would see him, but I knew Mom absolutely loved not only her brother, but his daughters as well. And she was extremely close to Aunt Ella. In fact, it took me awhile to figure out that he was the brother because she and Auntie were so much like blood sisters. They all were raised in Holly Springs together and their families were close. You don't know laughter until you've spent time with Aunt Ella and Mom! The two of them had stories about every subject on the face of the earth; and they had more experiences together than one could have in three lifetimes. Just a look or a wink and they were doubled over, rolling with laughter. And just being in their presence made you laugh. They were like two peas in a pod. Like Lucy Ricardo and Ethel Mertz. Like Queen Latifah and Jada Pinkett-Smith. Like peanut butter and jelly.

I have a deep and strong spiritual belief system and I cling to the Word of God, the Bible. It is my adoption experience that makes God so real to me. There was nothing I could have done to promote myself or to advocate for myself. Dr. Smith chose me. Mom and Daddy chose me. And God chose me. And God chooses all His children to be phenomenal, to show forth His love, and to do His good pleasure. So many times, Christians feel - and try to force others to feel - that if they are "good" enough, God will choose them. Our best can never be good enough. He just loves us. That's the first song I ever learned.

I'm told that I came home on a Thursday. The adoption agency, Mom told me, implored her to ease me into society, to keep me away from people until I got used to being in public. I'm so glad Mom ignored that suggestion. That first Saturday I went to church. My mother attended the Ephesus Seventh-day Adventist church on the Sabbath, which we observed from sundown on Friday to sundown on Saturday. I always believed that the Sabbath was designed just for women, because we don't cook, do laundry or any other kind of housework on that day. All preparations are completed before the sun goes down on Friday. That first Sabbath I went to Sabbath School, which is like Sunday School, and learned a song that I would sing over and over throughout my life. The song went like this:

Jesus loves me, this I know!
For the Bible tells me so.
Little ones to Him belong
They are weak, but He is strong.

CHORUS:
Yes, Jesus loves me!
Yes, Jesus loves me!
Yes, Jesus loves me!
For the Bible tells me so.

Little did I know that this simple song would carry me through many a trial. It was in Sabbath School that I also met other children my age – Rosalind, Leroy, Vickie, and Ethel. They all were the "babies" of their large families. Any family with more than one child in it was large to me! Rosalind was my closest friend growing up. We would spend many hours together playing and sharing our hopes and dreams. She was the youngest of seven. Now that I think about it, I guess that IS a large family! As time passed, I would get to know more and more people.

Ephesus was a close-knit, loving church family and anyone who walked into those doors was part of that family. I've always kept in touch with its members and will keep them ever in my prayers and thoughts. Because our church was small, every talent was needed and appreciated. We could do things well because we had practiced at the little church on the corner of Wadsworth and 20th. We have grown up and done great things, and I am convinced that it is because of the nurture and care that we received in that fellowship. It didn't take long for me to find my place in our church and I was accepted from the start. Everyone was my "aunt", "uncle" "brother" or "sister" and they all seemed to really love my mother. She was known for being a gracious hostess, a great cook and an excellent baker. Many Sabbaths would find our home brimming with people, especially the youth. Ours was a great home for budding romances. I watched courtships bloom, flourish and have witnessed their love remaining strong throughout all seasons of life. But not just our home. Plenty of the other members opened their homes as well. As a teenager, we could easily stay out on the weekends until 2:00 and 3:00 am fellowshipping at members' homes. We didn't need to worry about curfew violations. We were safe, happy and content.

CHAPTER FIVE

The Most Beautiful Girl in the World

It seems that my appearance on the scene caused quite a stir. Neighbors were curious and anxious to meet the new little Jones girl. My first visitor, who came to our home just hours after we arrived home, was "Aunt Kathy". She, her husband, "Uncle Don," and children, Ron and Terri, lived three houses down from us on Moton Drive. Technically they were right next door, as the two houses in between our lots had not been built yet. Aunt Kathy and mom were neighbors and we also attended the same church. Most importantly, they were dear friends. Mom often told me how Aunt Kathy couldn't wait to meet me, but when she got to our home, I was napping. Aunt Kathy peeked in on me, asleep in my very own bed in my very own room, and instantly nicknamed me, "Ruby." How I loved to hear her speak that nickname to me! She would call me that precious name for the rest of her life.

I don't remember meeting Aunt Kathy, it seems like she had always been there. But I do remember meeting Terri. In my eyes, then as well as now, Terri was the most beautiful girl in the world. Physically she was tall, shapely and gorgeous. Her skin the color of coffee with four creams in it; beautiful brown eyes, and hair that was long and thick. She had what I considered to be a perfect smile and her nails looked as if the top salon in the nation had created them, but I knew full well that she grew them all by herself, since I was a nail-biter. Her age had not hit double digits when I first met her, and I thought she was sheer perfection.

More than that, Terri was extremely kind to me. Like a loving big sister, you know? In fact, for many years, I considered her to be my only sister in the whole wide world. But really, to be honest, she was kind to everyone. After all these years I can still remember what it felt like to have someone treat me like they cared. I suppose, now that I think about it, she was really my first mentor, and I didn't even know it. It was not rare to find her reading to me before I learned to love reading for myself, or later explaining homework concepts to me, and still later sharing her limitless knowledge with me. I was indeed blessed to have her in my circle, and I knew that from the very beginning of my life on Moton Drive.

I had the biggest crush on Ron, who always treated me like a kid sister, much to my disappointment. It didn't take me long to figure out that our "relationship", which was completely created in my own mind, wasn't going to work and so I hastily "moved on."

Every June, Aunt Kathy and Mom, Ron and Terri and I would go to a spiritual encampment together and we would make the almost three-hour trek to Cassopolis, Michigan for a ten-day retreat. Our fathers would remain at home, but made sure that we had everything we needed for our vacation. We would plan all year for this special time and went together each summer for many years. Sometimes we would stay in a cabin by the lake, but most times we would haul a trailer up to the sacred grounds. Our camp meeting adventures could fill a book all its own, and many precious memories were made during that time. While at camp meeting, activities were planned according to age, so I was never in a meeting with Terri or Ron, but we would have evening meals together and share the fun things we had done during the day. I loved those times. While I never really minded being an only child, it felt wonderful to feel that I was part of a family with other children in it. Each year when we went to Cassopolis, I felt like I had siblings. And I loved the time that I spent with the most beautiful girl in the world.

It would be at a camp meeting during the summer I was turning ten, that a boy would tell me I was beautiful. That was a hard concept for me to wrap my mind around. Oh, I thought I was okay looking. And I had received plenty of compliments about being pretty or even "nice looking." Not to mention the fact that my Daddy told me all the time that I was pretty and that I could do anything I wanted to do in the whole wide world. But beautiful? No. That description belonged only to Terri; not me! Yet I remember thinking that if someone thought I was beautiful, then I was going to do everything I could to prove him right. I watched Terri, studied her really, and tried to imitate her mannerisms, voice, walk and movements, since in my mind she was beauty personified. However, it didn't take long at all for me to realize that I simply could not be like the most beautiful girl in the world. I had to be exactly who I was. I recognized Terri had always accepted me, just as I was. She never tried to change me, or to make me feel inferior or less than. She was someone on whom I could depend.

I will be forever grateful to you, Terri, and if you are reading this, know that "Jonesy," (her nickname for me) still admires and respects you. There simply aren't enough "thank you's" in the world to express how much I appreciate your treatment of me during those early, uncertain years of my life. You will never know what your simple kindness meant to me all those years ago. But maybe someone reading these words will understand how important it is to be kind to everyone. Kindness equals beauty, and it always will.

I still praise God for plucking me from the barren lands of the orphanage and planting me in the field of Moton Drive. If you grew up on that street in the '60s and '70s, you were one of the blessed ones. The day we pulled into the driveway of my home is the day I saw a curly-headed boy with a great big smile. It didn't take long for Jai Haithco to ring our doorbell, for he wanted to know more about the little girl he saw riding in the front seat of that old Chevrolet. Jai and I became fast friends, and at the time, we were the smallest kids on the block. We did everything together! Back then we did not look at games as boy games and girl games, just games that we played that allowed us time to spend with each other. During those next few years I learned how to jump rope, ride a bike, and play all kinds of games from pick up sticks to jacks to tag and four-square, which we played in the middle of the street.

Our street was located between 19th and 21st, but wasn't named 20th. I thought that's what made us even more special and unique. Since it was a new development, there were open fields between the houses on this short street. The main cross streets were Lapeer and Janes, but our street curved horseshoe style from Lapeer to 19th. In other words, you could readily find our street from the Lapeer side, but if you were on Janes side, the streets went from 19th to 21st, and sort of tucked us away. Jai's house was right in the curve and could be seen from either side of the horseshoe. My house could only be seen from the Lapeer side.

I learned many life lessons as I played on the streets of Moton Drive. I learned to love all kinds of people, and accept them for who they were. In addition to the "traditional" family units, there were other families in the neighborhood, family raising their relatives, step parenting, and some whom we are still not sure what the relationship was. Still our families were close-knit, and we looked out for each other. As a young child, I was not permitted to leave our street, not even around to the part of the horseshoe that was still considered Moton Drive. I could go as far as the Haithco's house on one end and down to Lapeer on the other end. That was it. And yet I did not feel restricted at all. I was content and thrilled with my newfound freedom. I can't imagine that I ever went outdoors much when I lived at the orphanage. During the early days, I never allowed my mind to return there.

Jumping rope came easy to me; but Double Dutch had a rhythm all its own. It would take my visiting cousins from Chicago to truly teach me that fine art, but once I learned it, I felt that I could conquer the world! I would rock back and forth with the two moving ropes to get my timing exact. I had learned to watch the back rope, jumping in "back doors" when the rope was going away from me as opposed to twirling toward me. I learned that responding to what was right in front of me was not always the best way to tackle a problem. Watching that back rope was the key to success in double Dutch and in life.

Jai and I spent countless hours either on the porch or in the driveway playing the game of jacks. We knew there were ten rounds to jacks, and we knew how to play them all, although not by name. It would be years later before I would learn "doghouse" "around the world" "jump the fence" and all the skills of the game. What I did learn, however, was that life was a balancing act. Whenever we could flip all ten jacks over to the back of our hands and then again to the palm of our hands without dropping one, we could advance to the next round. Whoever got through all ten rounds first was the winner. Life is a balancing act and rare are the times when everything "flips" perfectly in one's hand. Usually we are bound to drop a few jacks here and there, but we can continue to play the game. Years later I stood at my kitchen sink in Grove City, Ohio, feeling overwhelmed and wondering if I would be able to hold onto any of the jacks in my hand. My mind went back to those simple days of my childhood and I wondered if I'd ever make it through the night. That particular day was a day where I saw no future, no sunshine, and no color.

Four square was a fun street game for us. Initially I got out all the time, not being quick enough to respond to that bouncing ball. But it didn't take long for me to master that game and become a formidable opponent in the game of Four square. This game taught me that it's hard to remain number one, and there is always someone waiting to take your place. You must continually guard your accomplishments or else you will find yourself waiting in line like all the rest.

When I was about seven years old, my parents bought me a 26" blue bike because I had outgrown my little red bike with the training wheels. How well do I remember my dad taking me outside to the sidewalk and running beside me as he steadied me on that bike. "Don't let me go!" I'd yell only to look back and discover Daddy had let me go and I was pedaling on my own. Sometimes I'd fall just because I looked back. Sometimes I'd fall at the thought of my Daddy not holding on to me. But before I knew it, I was soaring through the streets. I was born for bike riding. So, I got the huge bike and my parents had faith enough to believe that I could handle it. Well, handle it, I did. That bike was soon known as one of the fastest bikes on the street and I could not believe that I was winning bike races, even against some of the bigger boys. I learned that I had the capacity to do all kinds of things that I never thought possible and that my Heavenly Father was watching over me and protecting me, even when it felt like He's totally let go of my bicycle.

During the summers we would play outside from early in the morning until the street lights came on. We didn't worry about sun screen or bottled water or any kind of electronic device. We just played with each other, used our imaginations and took each challenge as it came our way. Sometimes, especially in the middle of the summer, we would play school with the other neighbor children. We would choose a teacher, create makeshift desks and find a book or two from which to study. By the time we began to play school, we all knew it must be time for us to return there. Jai and I never ran out of things to say, of fun things to do and of places to explore. We were always off on some far-away adventure, sailing the world to parts unknown, building forts and facing giants. Our imaginations were keen and carefree. The sky was the limit. In fact, I'm sure we rocketed to the moon and beyond on several of our excursions.

Time and life would drift us far away from each other, but grief would reunite us. It was my humble privilege to attend Jai's mother's funeral. Not too many years later, he escorted me down that lonely aisle at Mom's funeral. Other losses through the years caused us to connect in some way, and I am proud of the man he has become. It seems so fitting that this loving soul would become a leader of souls, a true minister of the gospel of Christ. May God's richest blessings remain upon your life, dear life-long friend, Reverend Dr. Jai S. Haithco, Sr.

CHAPTER SIX

The Best Part of My School Day was Recess

All too soon it was time for me to start school. I went to a half-day kindergarten at Morley Elementary School, which was at the end of our street. Jai and I started school at the same time, but we were in different classrooms, which made me very sad. I'm convinced school would have been much more fun if Jai and I had been in the same room and I don't remember much of kindergarten other than it was the most boring part of my day. To go there and watch these little children learn the letter "A" was unbearable for me. I, after all, could read. And so could my friends. What a waste of my time! I don't remember my teachers' names but I do remember getting into trouble for refusing to drink spoiled milk with my graham crackers one day. The teacher threatened that if I didn't drink my milk I wouldn't be able to plant flowers in a carton. Who cared? I certainly didn't. I didn't want to plant flowers at my own house; why in the world would I care to plant them at school? My punishment was to lie on my blanket while the other children got their hands dirty. What a fantastic "Punishment"! I was so ready for some "real" education!

For my first through ninths grades, I would be attending a "church" school that was located way out by the airport. It was even further away than the sugar beet factory, and I had to ride a bus to get there. The day before the first day of school, I got violently ill with a fever, chills, and vomiting. I was told I had the flu, which made no sense to me at all because I knew that only birds flew. But the grown-ups insisted that I had it, and I would miss the first week of school. I was so disappointed, but what could I do?

After a week of recuperation, I was declared fit and ready to face the world. The night before my official first day of school I could hardly sleep, I was so excited. My school was about 17 miles away and I would ride a huge yellow school bus to and from Tri City Junior Academy Seventh-day Adventist School for the next nine years. A group of dedicated parents drove us to a location far from home where the bus driver would pick us up, continue the route and pick up many others to take to school. We rode over an hour each way every day. My cousin, Ruthie, was living with us at that time and was in the tenth grade. Our entire school consisted of three classrooms, two restrooms, and an office for the principal. That was it. Ruthie's classroom had the high schoolers, grades nine and ten, and this was her last year before going on to public high school. The last room, grades five through eight, was taught by the principal. My class, grades one through four, was taught by the principal's wife. Multi-level grades can benefit all the children if it is done right and my teacher knew how to do it right. I loved Mrs. LeAnne Herbel, my teacher for all my four years in that same room. We didn't have a uniform per se, but we had to kneel in front of a one-inch-thick board every morning. If our skirts swept the top of the board or hung over it, we were fine, but if that skirt hovered above the top of that menacing board, we were to either pull our skirt down or find another dress to wear. It didn't matter to me as a first grader, but in later years I would hastily roll my skirt up after I knelt by that board. I was, after all, raised in the 60's and miniskirts were all the rave!

My first-grade class was the largest in our classroom; there were eight of us. I still remember all their full names plus all the names of their siblings. By the time we graduated from the eighth grade, we still had eight students in our class, although one left and was replaced by another. We knew each other well. There was only one other girl in my class and we spent those nine years as the only two girls in the class. I've only seen her a few times since we left Tri City, but now, in the age of Facebook, we have reconnected.

Racism and discrimination reared their ugly heads from the first day I attended school. Several of the white children asked me if I was dirty, if my stomach was the same color as my face and why didn't I take a bath every day. I was confused and unsure of what they meant; my mom was insistent on cleanliness. My clothing was new and Mom had pressed them better than any dry cleaners could ever do. Apparently, I was the only African-American girl they had ever seen. Back then we were still called "colored people" and I would be the only person of color in my grade for the entire nine years. The whole school had fewer than 50 students in it, but we were clearly in the minority. I could count "us" on one hand. Over the years I would disprove many stereotypes about people of color. It confused me that there were other Christians who thought that we were somehow less than human, that we didn't have the right to belong. But I remember two families in particular who learned a lot about the races and their own prejudices from me.

In one family, the grandmother, who was raising her deceased daughter's children, insisted that she would faint if she touched one of "us." She volunteered at the school far too much for my taste and she never missed an opportunity to warn us to stay away from her and not to touch her, lest she die. How I wanted to run up to her and rub against her, but I feared I'd be charged with murder. So, I kept my distance and did my best to never brush up against her. Mom, however, was determined to see what would happen if she touched us. So, Mom would reach out to shake her hand, which would cause her to recoil, draw her hand back and clutch it unto herself as if Mom were a rattle snake. But not to be deterred, Mom finally touched her, more than once, and would say, "Oh yeah? I'd like to see exactly what your reaction is going to be!" every time the lady insisted that she couldn't touch us. The lady would breathe rapidly and start sweating, but it certainly wasn't because of Mom's touch. Although, I suppose in many ways it was. Mom always made me laugh when she would try to touch the woman, but she clearly proved that "Mrs. Grandma" would not faint from touching us, try as she might.

Another family had three young sons, but their daughter was one grade above mine. She invited me for a sleepover, which my father, at first, refused to let me attend. "Children should be in their own beds when the lights go out," he insisted. But Mom convinced him that it wouldn't harm me to get to know my classmates. After all, by now I was in the third grade, and old enough to "handle myself", meaning I could bathe and dress myself without too much assistance. So, reluctantly, very reluctantly, my parents gave permission for me to go to Shelly's home. (not her real name) All of us travelled quite a distance to go to school, as the "Tri City" represented Midland, Bay City and Saginaw. I don't recall anything spectacular about her home other than they had to climb the stairs when it was bedtime. Children don't usually care about knick-knacks and furniture arrangements; they just want to have fun and spend time together.

During the night, I woke up to find Shelly staring at me, but I quickly rolled over and went back to sleep. Those who know me best know that I am a sound sleeper and nothing interrupts my sleeping. In fact, I did not even hear my newborn babies crying years later. The next morning, while eating breakfast, Shelly declared, "Daddy! You lied to me! I stayed up all night long watching Ruth-Ann, and she never grew a tail all night long!" I was stunned, embarrassed. I now understood why she had a sudden interest in befriending me and had insisted on inviting me home to spend the night. I looked around the table to find horrified faces on the mother and brothers and downright shame on father's face. That was the first time I noticed that faces could turn red. He looked like a stop light! The other details of the morning are a blur, but I do remember waiting a long time for the bus to arrive that morning, which probably means we were scurried out of that house faster than the speed of sound!

I couldn't wait to get home and tell Daddy what happened! When I told him, Daddy's response surprised me: "I'm sorry that happened to you, Ruth-Ann, but there's nothing you can do to change someone's opinion of you. Just be yourself; that's who God made you to be." Daddy never spoke of that incident again, at least not to me. But from that day to this one, every time I see Shelly's father, he cannot look me in the eye! He had tried to spread fear and hatred, but his attempts failed. Shelly is now a physician, and I pray that she treats all her patients with dignity and respect, no matter what they look like or where they come from. And I'm sure her extensive medical studies taught her humans do not grow tails at night!

I absolutely, positively loved my recess time at Tri City Junior Academy. Recess was twice a day and then again during our lunch time. Never had I spent that much time in such wide-open spaces with so many choices. It was my delight to spend time outside in that vast expanse of a yard. When the doors opened for recess on my first day of school, I couldn't decide which way to turn. A graveled parking lot gave way to what had to be acres of green grass. There were areas to play football and softball. All the childhood outdoor play equipment was available. And if we ever got bored or adventurous, there was an old covered well way out at the end of the property, almost to the fence. Whoever designed this school understood children needed lots of open field to run and explore. Any time I was outside was by far my favorite time of the day.

I learned so much about life from recesses at Tri City. The first stop I made on day one was the Merry-Go-Round. I had never seen anything so mesmerizing in my life. It went around and around and around … and I had no idea how to get on or off. Some of the bigger kids showed me exactly what to do. I had to get a running start, moving in rhythmic speed of the Merry-Go-Round, and then jump on it. Sometimes that Merry-Go-Round sat motionless and we could just get on it without effort, but it still took the manpower of running to get it going and it took so much more energy to get that equipment moving from a stopped position. It didn't take long to figure out that I needed to connect with someone who was moving and actively doing something for themselves, and that trying to do anything with someone who wasn't already moving themselves was the most difficult thing to do. I also learned that motion doesn't always mean progress – we went around and round for years and never moved from that same spot on the playground.

We had hours and hours of non-stop fun in that school yard. We played on the Monkey Bars, the Slide, and learned all the rules of Tether Ball. We would sometimes run around that huge playground just for the sheer pleasure of feeling the wind in our faces. In the bitter cold of the Michigan winters, we would make blocks out of the snow and build our own forts, complete with rooms and tunnels and areas to keep us shielded from the wind. We would jump rope and hop scotch and even create new games. There was always something to do and someone to play with and if all else failed, we used our imaginations. We would venture out to the "Old Well in the Field by the Fence" and invent stories about people who lived long ago.

Turning six years old also meant I now had to take piano lessons. Mom couldn't hold a tune in a bucket, but loved music and had always wanted to play the piano. It would be mandatory that her daughter knew how to tickle the ivory keys. It was the only time I could walk around the horseshoe by myself because my music teacher lived on the corner of 19th Street and Janes.

Riley Dennett was a confirmed bachelor who lived with his grandmother. Or maybe she lived with him, I'm not sure. His black and white split-level home housed three pianos and two organs. Maybe more. And he was left-handed. I remember that because I would watch him write notes for me or receipts to give to Mom. He was tall, and his back held his body as straight as a board. Piano lessons were another thing that I hated so much. How I wish I had paid more attention when learning scales and whatever else I wasn't paying attention to at the time. I took lessons from Mr. Dennett for eleven years and can only play three songs from memory. What a shame! I can, however, sight-read just about anything, and now that I'm on "the back side of 40" I love that I can play the piano, although certainly not as well as I could have had I put a little more effort into it.

Music didn't come easy for me though, and I hated the time spent in practice. However, years later, as I was earning my court reporting degree, I would use the same discipline that I learned during that time. Mom had me get up early in the morning and put in an hour of practice before we left for school. I felt like I was banished to outer darkness when I was in that basement in the wee hours of the morning. Those were the only times when I dreaded going down there. Somehow, I made my way through those rehearsals and I am the better for it. Two of my children wanted to take piano lessons, and I regret not letting them do it. I just hated it so much that I couldn't bear to put my children through the rigors of tedious practice. I'm sure that the minute they showed signs of wearying, I would have caved in and told them that they didn't have to do it. Hindsight teaches me that I should have allowed them to at least try.

CHAPTER SEVEN

Put Me Down and Let Me Walk...
'cause You're Carrying Me Too Fast!

O nce I completed the ninth grade, I was ready to attend a boarding academy, also affiliated with our denomination. In this school, I was again in the minority. Cedar Lake Academy (CLA) was in Cedar Lake, Michigan, about an hour's drive from our home. Of the over 300 students in attendance, there were only 12 black students. We weren't referring to ourselves as African American yet. It would be a few months and a few more trials before we realized that the school did not believe in mixing the races. There were also plenty of parents who either did not want us there or, more importantly, did not want their children to room with us.

However, my roommate, Carolyn Salisbury, had parents who not only wanted us to room together, but encouraged it. Carolyn was a tiny little thing, blonde haired and green eyed. She could unlock any door, jumpstart any car and drive it whether manual, some call a stick shift, or automatic. I had met Carolyn years before when, for reasons that I will never understand, I signed up for gymnastics camp at the beautiful Camp Au Sable, situated on 840 acres of land that curved around Shellenbarger Lake near Grayling, Michigan.

Apparently, Carolyn had made the same mistake. Together we were the official goofballs of the gymnastic camp, bumbling and stumbling, aching and scraping through that entire week, but I was so grateful to have someone else with me who also had no clue about the logistics of gymnastics. We both thought the same way; this would be a camp for those interested in performing light acrobatic stunts. Instead we quickly discovered that it was a camp for those who were aspiring to take their skills to the next level. We spent an hour per day at each of these stations: the parallel bars, the uneven bars, the balance beam, floor exercises, the rings that hung high from the gymnasium's roof along with plenty other torturous twists, flips and turns that neither of us had the skillset for in the least. Carolyn and I got close during those times when our instructors would frustratingly scoot us to the side while they coached the REAL athletes. It was during that time that we learned a lot about each other and discovered that we would both attend Cedar Lake at the very same time. We vowed then to be roommates.

True to the camp brochure's promise, we were incorporated into the grand finale given to the adoring parents on Saturday night. Carolyn and I came out in our festive garb, knelt gingerly on one knee and extended our arms up toward the heavens. There we remained until intermission. For the second half of the show, we knelt on the opposite knee, extended our opposite arms and smiled. The gymnasts flipped and twirled over our heads with grace and finesse and our parents were as proud of our accomplishments as if we were the latest protégées slated for Olympic recognition. It was also fortunate that the two sets of parents sat together during the performance. They became fast friends.

During the months and years ahead, we spent time at each other's homes, chose our bedding and curtains for our room and mailed plenty of letters back and forth. This was before the days of Facebook and email, and we had to rely on the trusty mailman to keep our communication alive. Each week I would write a letter to Carolyn and received one from her. That correspondence was filled with hopes and dreams, frustrations and enjoyments, ups and downs and everything in between. It's amazing what a pen and paper and a little private time can do for young ladies embarking upon the teen years. All the things I dared not say to parents and would-be suitors, I said in those letters. And Carolyn did the same. We learned an extremely large amount about each other during those four years and our resolve never changed.

I was so excited that she was going to be my roommate and when we sent in our applications, we listed each other's names on the form. We were required to send in pictures as well; but neither of us had a spare one at the time. With a name like Ruth-Ann Jones, who would be attending CLA from Tri-City Intermediate School (we had undergone a name change in my nine years there), it was assumed that I, too, was Caucasian. That's the only way the two of us got the opportunity to room together.

It would take about two months for the dean to realize that she had a situation on her hands. Black and white were rooming together, and that was not to be tolerated! Since, in her words, we "all look alike," she was seeing me and incorrectly assumed I was another girl in the dorm. Once she realized her "error," she immediately called, not my parents, but Carolyn's, to apologize and offer a "remedy" to the "problem." Mr. Salisbury was emphatic. We girls were to room together and no one was to break us apart! The dean would try several other tricks to separate us, ultimately threatening Carolyn to not be able to live on the upper classman wing during her senior year, which by then, we were both upperclassman and should have been upstairs. So, we spent her last year on the sophomore wing of the girls' dorm, happy as ever to be there.

The world was not ready for Carolyn Dale Salisbury. She had our room rigged so that when the lights went out nightly at 10:00 pm, ours remained on. Of course, we had to monitor that closely, lest we be discovered, but she knew how to make anything work. It would be Carolyn's adventurous spirit that led us to the cafeteria through an underground tunnel. We would go over there and find lemonade, ice cream or other culinary delights and help ourselves to them during the boring evenings. She always made me laugh, was a hard worker and was passionate about those whom she loved. I was more than blessed to have her as a roommate for two years at CLA.

It was while I was a sophomore at CLA that the TV mini-series, "Roots" made its debut. It was a dramatization of author Alex Haley's family line from ancestor Kunta Kinte's enslavement to his descendant's liberation and depicted the worst of times in America's history where people of color were discounted and mistreated. The horrors of slavery were brought to life in this movie and somehow, we could watch it in the guest room of the girls' dorm. Those images are forever ingrained in my mind, and it was then that everything my grandparents and parents had tried to instill in me was understood. Most of my classmates tried to excuse the actions of the slave owners, giving frail excuses and dismissing that time as "in the past" and insisting that we should just "move on from here." But not Carolyn.

Culturally aware and sensitive, she listened, empathized and vowed that she would teach her children to accept everyone as equal. My Caucasian friend understood, and it meant the world to me.

Later, however, she would choose to marry a bigoted and hate-filled partner. And life would not be kind to this awesome and love-filled soul.

My high school days were filled with adventure. I loved dorm life which was a new adventure for an only child. As part of a work-study program, I worked several part-time jobs, including cafeteria cook's helper and English department secretary during my three years at Cedar Lake Academy. I joined the Academy Choir. I ultimately became part of the academy's first all African-American Junior and Senior Trio, singing with Reneé Logan and Linda Carpenter with her sister, Regenia accompanying us. We spent countless hours practicing and performing all over the state of Michigan. Reneé, whom we called "Logan," started a drill team – also an academy first – and we performed various routines in perfect formation under her strict direction. It was during my time at CLA that I met my life-long "little sister" Reneé Scruggs. We called her Scruggs. Her parents brought her from Detroit to Saginaw, and she rode with us to the academy. Those trips bonded us for life. She has endured much in life, including the loss of her left leg at the age of 18, and has become a fierce advocate for persons with disabilities.

Other talents and gifts were magnified during that time. It seemed fitting that I became a reporter for The Cedar Log school newspaper. I honed my leadership and organizational skills as Girls' Dorm president my junior year and class vice president my senior year. My Mom and Daddy were only an hour away, but the other parents visited routinely as well, and their parents became like family to us. When they brought food, it was usually enough to share with us all. I felt supported and loved.

Our principal, Robert LeBard, whom I affectionately called "Uncle Bob" had an open-door policy, and I treasured my conversations with him. He was so unlike the majority of the faculty members at CLA. I was unable to detect even a hint of racism or elitism with him. He didn't refer to us as "you people" or make assumptions about our inability to excel. He was a tall man with a huge, giving heart and I am blessed to have spent time in his presence.

May 28, 1978 was the graduation date that ended my high school career. Although others assumed this would happen, I was genuinely surprised and elated when Daddy handed me a congratulatory card with keys and Polaroid pictures of my very own car. It was a 1974 fire engine red Gremlin with denim interior. I promptly named it "Levi." Those high school years flew by and I felt that the world was moving faster than I wanted it to move. Aunt Ella used to say, "Put me down and let me walk, 'cause you're carrying me too fast!"

CHAPTER EIGHT

Got the World in a Jug... and the Stopper in My Hand!

My high school guidance counselor insisted I was well suited for a housekeeping job at a local hotel. Good hours, she said, and plenty of work to keep me busy. She did not base her recommendation on my academic history or my love for vacuuming, but because she was convinced "blacks don't make good workers in any other field." She strongly discouraged me from even seeking entrance into an institution of higher learning – all of this, even though I was an Honor Roll student throughout my academic years.

In my family, going to college was rarely discussed and certainly not something to which one would aspire, but I am so grateful that I didn't take the guidance counselor's advice. My father had completed 12th grade but did not graduate because he had to begin working to help support his family. Mom finished the 8th grade and did no more schooling, which was commonplace in her day. Daddy Frank and Momma Anna had only completed the 4th grade, which was considered exceptional for farmers back in the early 1900's. So, the fact that I had graduated from high school with honors was a pretty big deal in my family. My parents were extremely proud of me, and would have been happy if I had started working then.

But I didn't feel like going to work right away, even though I was sure to get the $17.00 an hour line assembly job at a General Motors foundry. I wanted more out of life at the age of 17. Because of the wonderful retirement benefits Daddy received, I could attend any college in the state of Michigan, public or private, at no cost to our family. And because Daddy insisted on private schools, I chose to go to Andrews University, a Seventh-day Adventist college founded in 1874, located in Berrien Springs, Michigan. Since I loved to write and had been a roving reporter for The Cedar Log, it made sense to me that I would choose Communications as my major with an English minor.

The schedule was nice – classes from 7:00 to 11:00 am – and the rest of the day I was completely free. I can't say exactly what it was that caused me to feel so restless at Andrews, but I suppose I had too much time on my hands. I suppose I thought I'd have plenty of time to get my school work completed. I suppose that during my car runs to South Bend, Indiana, with Kenneth, a friend who went on to become a well-known actor in film and television, I got a taste for life outside of Michigan. I suppose it was the fact that I was now attending college with the same kids I had been with from first to ninth grade, but those same classmates didn't seem to recognize me now that we were in college. Whatever it was, after just one quarter I told my parents I did not want to return to Andrews. Although my tuition was free, I simply hated my Andrews experience. The work was not difficult; however, my grades were a solid "C" average. This was the first time my grades or my spirits had ever been that low. Mom wanted me to stay; she liked having me only three and a half hours away from her, but thankfully Daddy heard my heart.

January of 1979 we piled into the car and took the 700-mile journey down to Oakwood College (now Oakwood University). I could not believe that I was standing on the campus of Oakwood College, a 380-acre former slave plantation, established by the SDA church in 1896. It was founded to educate African Americans in the South. The campus was spectacular to me and just driving onto it reminded me of those years long ago when I arrived at the house on Moton Drive. I felt like I was home. We got there at 3:30 in the morning and just picked a random dorm to enter, since we had never been there before. We were met by a beautiful young lady wearing curlers in her hair the size of soup cans. I had never known anyone with hair long enough to accommodate such curlers and I couldn't keep my eyes off her. She welcomed us warmly and offered us temporary lodging until the office opened. Little did I know that Cindy Mitchell (now Washington) would become a dear friend to me, that we would live in the same cities of Columbus and Pittsburgh, and that our children would grow up together.

The registration process was easy because there were only a few of us registering. Mom and Daddy helped me settle in to my room but it would be much later in the day that I would meet my roommate, Gail. When my parents headed for home, I was convinced that I had made the right decision and was grateful they helped me on this portion of my journey.

I only knew a few people down there, three to be exact, Reneé, Linda and Tina, but Oakwood quickly became the place of many of my fondest memories. At that time, Oakwood only offered Communications as a minor, so I switched to an English major. Because I had transferred in the middle of the school year, I had to play catch-up with meeting people and getting involved in activities, but it certainly didn't take me long to adjust.

Oakwood College did so much for me. I immediately joined the college choir and was hired part time in the nursing department. My days were full, my grades were great, and my heart was content. Imagine life before the days of cell phones, or even phones in our rooms, yet somehow, we girls managed a routine of sharing this precious commodity. I spoke to my parents once a week on the hallway pay phone. Every time we talked, they could tell by my voice that I was extremely happy and they could hear sheer joy leaping through the telephone lines. I felt as if Oakwood was a second home for me. Students felt like family. I loved the worship services, and my classes were engaging and informative. It would be the first time in my academic career that I loved learning. The teachers were invested in our education and encouraged us to reach for the academic stars. Excellence was not just required, it was expected and every resource was made available to us. When I looked around, others looked just like me and saw my potential as far more than the hired help. I could inhale deeply and fill my lungs with positivity and love.

Most of my friends stayed in either my dorm, Peterson Hall, or Cunningham Hall, which were the underclassmen female dorms at that time. I had no desire to venture past the library to visit Edwards Hall or "Gentlemen's Estates" which were the two male dorms on campus. Meals were served in the cafeteria, and while many complained about the food, I really enjoyed eating there. I had "café buddies," people whom I only saw during meals, and after a while I spent most breakfasts with Phil. Because we shared the same last name, I always considered him to be a "cousin." Tall, dark and handsome, he was pleasant and easy to talk with, and I came to enjoy our purely platonic relationship.

I went on dates with a few guys but was really focused on "doing my thing." It amazed me that there were so many possible career options and talking to other students inspired me beyond my wildest imaginations. My days were filled and I met people from everywhere. I loved my life and enjoyed my studies immensely.

Spring of 1979, Tina and I returned from our home leave very late and could not register for the classes we originally intended to take. I knew I needed a math class and was determined to stay on course for graduation, but the class for the beloved Dr. Blake, head of the mathematics department, was filled. Both Tina and I were sorely disappointed. Our second and third choices were filled as well, which left only one math teacher left, Mr. Tim Williams. Relatively new to the college, he was known for being harsh and inflexible. No one wanted to take his class! But we were desperate.

"Sorry, my class is full," he said matter-of-factly.

But then I proposed a plan. "What if you sign our paperwork and we attend class on the very first day?" I posed a question. "Since people usually drop their classes or don't attend on that first day, there will probably be openings for us. So, if your class is full, and all these people on the roster come, we will drop the class. But if not, we will stay in the class, and I assure you, we won't drop it!"

Mr. Williams shrugged his shoulders, signed on the appropriate line, and we had now completed registration for the Spring Quarter.

Within a few weeks, I went on a choir trip to Asheville, North Carolina. Now, initially I wasn't slated to go, but I continued to practice with the choir, thanks to great advice from Tina, and as people dropped out for one reason or another, I was able to fill a much-needed alto spot. While on the trip, I had the opportunity to interact socially with one of the chaperones, Mr. Tim Williams. I felt so at ease with him that I began calling him "Tim" on the trip. Conversation was easy with Tim and I soon found out his home town was Buffalo, New York. My mother had lived there, we had family there, and some of my newfound friends were from there as well. In class, he was staunch and stoic, but on this trip, he smiled easily and had a gentle way about him that was comfortable and relaxed. The choir trip was a great success and we all seemed to have such a great time.

Once we got back to campus, Tim offered Tina and I, and another choir member, Cheryl, a ride back to our dorm, which I thought was extremely gracious. Tina jokingly ribbed me in the side and declared, "Mr. Williams likes you!" I touted up my lips and smirked. "Oh, no he does not! We are just friends!" Who would ever think of liking your math teacher!

The next day in class, he handed back our papers, and there was a note written at the bottom of mine in red ink: *I would like to see you in my office. Mr. Williams.* When I showed it to Tina, she laughed and said, "See there! I told you he likes you!" But I was convinced that he was going to warn me to never call him "Tim" on campus. Later that day, I went to his office but there were lots of students in there and he asked me if I would return later. I went back the next day, and Tina was the only student in his office. She gave me a quick wink, gathered up her books and raced out of the room so fast I could barely say hello to her! So now there I was in Mr. Tim Williams' office. I braced for a stern reprimand.

"I'm going to Detroit this weekend," he began.

"So?" my response was quick and flippant.

"So ... I was wondering if you needed me to take something to your parents or pick up something for you. You did say you were from Michigan, right?"

His words threw me off guard but I managed to explain to him that Saginaw was 100 miles north of Detroit, and thanked him for the gracious offer. We talked for about 20 minutes. It was always easy to talk to Tim. So comfortable it was that he invited me to sit with him at Prayer Meeting the next evening. Not. At. All! At our school, whenever two people of the opposite sex joined each other for prayer meeting, it was a sign that they were dating, or at least very interested in one another. And I was certainly NOT dating my mathematics professor! After all, Tim had to be what? A hundred years old? At least!

"Well, will you at least go to Stanlieo's with me sometime?" Tim asked with a twinkle in his eye. Stanlieo's Sub Villa was the best sub shop in town, offering vegetarian and meat options with lots of toppings. I had only been there twice before and loved it both times. My hasty answer was, "Why, of course I will!" Before I left his office, I noticed his degrees mounted meticulously upon the wall. A bachelor's degree of mathematics from Oakwood College and a mathematical master's degree from Andrews University had been awarded to J. Timothy Williams. As I entered the hallway of Green Hall I wondered what the "J" stood for.

The next day I saw Tim both in class and at prayer meeting, where I was careful to sit on the complete opposite side of the church. Thursday in class I averted my eyes whenever he looked my way. By the weekend I had all but forgotten about him, the conversation and anything having to do with dating anyone. I had decided that I would buckle down on Sunday and get some much-needed studying accomplished. After going to breakfast early, sans shower, I raced back to the room to hit the books. Anyone who came knocking at my door found me deep in study and knew I wasn't going to be hanging with them that day. Around five o'clock I had just closed my books and rubbed my eyes when I heard a voice yell, "Ruth-Ann Jones, you have a phone call."

Convinced it was my parents, I ran to the phone and breathlessly answered, "Hello?"

A male voice was on the other end. "Hi. I'm back from my trip. How would you like to go to Stanlieo's?"

After a long pause, I said, "Uh, Tim?"

"Yes?" His voice sounded smooth and quite amused.

"Sure. I can go. What time will you be here to pick me up?"

"I'm in the lobby." I inhaled deeply and tried to not sound panicky. "Okay. Give me minute. And I'll be right down."

I slammed the phone down and went into turbo speed. Somehow, I managed to shower, brush teeth, do something with my unruly hair, assemble and iron my outfit and put on a hint of make up in record time. As I was in the midst of my whirlwind, my roommate raced into our room. "Mr. Williams is here!" she exclaimed! "That ffffiiiiiinnnneeee Mr. Williams is HERE! And he's gonna pick up somebody. I'm going back to Lu's room to see who it is!" And in a blur, she ran back out of the room and raced down the hallway.

Gathering myself and making sure that I had a quarter to call for a cab plus the cab fare if I needed it, I took a deep breath and exited my dorm room. Walking down the hallway, it seemed as if I were dreaming. When I reached the bottom step, I spotted Tim across the lobby. He was leaning on the office counter, watching me walk toward him.

"Hello," I was first to speak.

"Hi," he quietly responded.

I signed out of the dorm, a policy that must be strictly adhered to, and then he opened the door and we descended the stairs toward his waiting 1974 five-speed white mustang. As we were walking down the sidewalk, I could hear my roommate's voice echoing across the campus, "Ruth-Ann Jones! Well, I'll be #@$%!" I was 18 years old. Tim was 26.

After our first date at Stanlieo's, we sat together at prayer meeting the following Wednesday, and it became common knowledge that I was dating my math teacher. People stared, pointed and whispered, but few spoke to either of us directly. My close circle of friends were Tara, Gwen and Tina, and they knew from the beginning what was going on with me and Tim. I found them to be supportive, prayerful and wise, though they teased me often about dating "Father Time." All these years later, we have kept in touch and have recently committed to getting together once a year for a girls' weekend. I will be eternally grateful to them for their unconditional love.

Tim was my first real boyfriend, and I was young, naïve, and completely oblivious to the structural inequities of dating my teacher. In 1979 there were no policies in place to prohibit faculty/student dating, but it was clear that my classmates and most of his colleagues were not happy with our choice. However, Tim didn't play favorites in the classroom and was known to be an exacting and difficult instructor. I remember a time when a young man yelled across the campus, "Ruth-Ann Jones is f***ing the math teacher!" and I ran to my dorm in tears. That comment was extremely hurtful to me. At that time Tim and I had not even kissed, and I was a virgin. I have no idea how many, if any, complained about us to the administration. Plenty of people just shunned me which drew me even closer to the one who chose to spend time with me. Thankfully, the quarter was almost over when we began to date. By the way, I earned a B+ in that math class; Tina got an A.

I was never Tim's secret. He boldly spent time with me out in the open and proudly introduced me to his circle of friends. Our saving grace was the fact that Tim lived in a house with a woman who was on the staff of Oakwood. He introduced me to her the first week we were dating. Mrs. Dorothy Holloway Smith was a delightful woman, a consummate entertainer and reminded me of my own mother. We got along great and I loved working alongside her in the kitchen. Her culinary delights were amazing and many students and faculty placed their feet under her dining room table. She had an open-door policy and it was the perfect atmosphere for our courtship to blossom and grow. Many evenings we sat in her home playing board games and talking about every subject under the sun. You find out a lot about a person when you play simple games and have basic conversation, and I learned about Tim and his family during those times. We spent very little time alone but when we did, Tim always planned wonderful places for us to go. I enjoyed our dates tremendously.

One day Tim decided that it was time to "meet" his mother, so he called her and said, "Remember the girl I told you about? Well, she's here and I want you to speak to Ruth-Ann Jones." I nervously took the phone and timidly said, "Hello?"

"Don't get pregnant and trap my son into marrying you," were Naomi Williams' first words to me.

"Oh, that's not gonna happen," all my timidity had departed and now I was fiery mad.

"And please don't tell him what I said. He wouldn't like it," her tone turned to almost pleading.

"Oh, I'm tellin' as soon as I hang up this phone," I retorted and handed the phone back to him. He finished his conversation with her and came to find me. By now I had walked into the living room and was fuming.

"Before you say anything, I want you to know that my mother can be a little … brash. That's just how she is," he explained. "I know she said something offensive and I want to apologize on her behalf." When I told him what she said, he seemed genuinely upset. It was then I discovered he had a contentious relationship with his mother. And beginning right then, so did I! It would be decades of fights and arguments between "Naomi and Ruth" and I often joked that if the two of us had been the Naomi and Ruth of the Bible, it would read a completely different way! I never imagined I'd have such a contentious relationship with my mother-in-law, but I did. It would take many, many years before I would come to truly love and accept her just the way she was and hear her thank me for "always trying" with her.

We continued dating and getting to know one another. One day in class Tim was writing algebraic problems on the blackboard when a student yelled out, "Hey, Mr. Williams! What's your favorite candy bar?" Without hesitation Tim responded, "Baby Ruth," which sent the class into an eruption of laughter. Naturally I was mortified and ever so grateful that I sat in the very first row. Tim continued to teach at the blackboard, his back to the class for the remainder of the period. When the bell rang, I remained in my seat and never spoke a word. Once everyone was gone, he turned around, extended his arms, and said, "But Baby Ruth IS my favorite candy bar!" My fellow students began to refer to me as "Mr. Williams' favorite candy bar." We both got years of laughter out of that one.

We dated the rest of that spring quarter, parted ways for the summer but wrote letters often to each other. Those letters opened even more of our hearts to each other and when the new school year began, we continued our courtship. By now Tim had secured a small apartment on Faculty Road and had a roommate, Sherwin Jack. I nicknamed the room mates, "Sherwin Williams" like the paint store. Sherwin was an older student and soon to graduate as a theologian. He was extremely kind and quiet in his mannerisms. I liked him the moment I met him and through the years have admired him and his then-fiancée-now-wife Patricia.

Tim asked me to marry him in a simple way on January 3, 1980. We decided to get married on August 3, the day after my 20th birthday, so no one would ever say that I was a teen-age bride. I wanted a small, simple ceremony but my mother would have none of that. We ended up with ten bridesmaids and groomsmen and over 500 guests. In April of that year, my father was pumping gas when a car rolled back on him, damaging his leg severely. We were afraid he was going to lose that leg, but doctors managed to save it. When it got closer to the time for my wedding, Daddy was still walking with a cane, so Tim and I and our wedding coordinator, Mrs. Thelma Anderson, Tina's mom, decided to have our groomsmen wear top hats and carry canes. It added such class and flair to our wedding. Another great example of all things working together for good ...

My maid of honor was Tina. My matron of honor was Carolyn; I had been her maid of honor the year before. We were all so young! The wedding went off without a hitch and I couldn't have been happier to be Mrs. Jethro Timothy Williams. But this would be the last day that I would see Carolyn, my gymnastics-buddy-turned-roommate alive. In March of the following year she was brutally murdered by her husband. All these years later, it's still difficult to talk about. Thankfully she had a beautiful daughter that I have been blessed to watch grow up, marry and have a family of her very own. She doesn't remember her mother since she was only 14 months old when we lost Carolyn, but I still stand in prayerful watch over the child of my dear friend.

Tim taught at Oakwood one more year and in June of 1981, we relocated to the Columbus, Ohio area. He was chosen to be a systems analyst for Chemical Abstracts Service (CAS). He also enrolled in the mathematic doctoral studies program at The Ohio State University. By July, we discovered that I was pregnant and thankfully I found employment at CAS too, which worked out great for us, since by now we only had one car. "Levi" had stopped working soon after the honeymoon. How I missed that car! CAS was a great place to work and we made friends easily. The company offered "flex time," where we could go in as early as 6 am, take anywhere from 30 minutes to an hour and a half lunch and finish out our eight hours of working time. This schedule was perfect. We rode in to work together, ate lunch together and rode home together. To some that would be too much "togetherness," but it worked for us. Tim was truly my best friend. We never seemed to run out of things to talk about.

I was content in my life with Tim. Things were far from perfect, but I was doing all right. By now we had joined Ephesus SDA Church in Columbus and were slowly making connections and friendships there. Our circle of friends was small but close knit. There were social activities and many things to see and do in the city, which kept us busy and our lives full. During this time in my life, Mom would often say to me, "Ruth-Ann, you've got the world in a jug, and the stopper in your hand."

CHAPTER NINE

Created for Fruitfulness

Perhaps it was my personal desire all along or perhaps it was from knowing how much Mom desperately wanted children, but I knew that I wanted to have lots of children. Tim and I had decided that we would have at least two, possibly three. Our plan was to wait until he finished his PhD, then I would return to school to finish my bachelor's and beyond. And how God laughs at our plans.

Ten months into our marriage I discovered I was pregnant with our first son. The first order of business was to find a doctor, and Dr. Donald Bryan's office was conveniently located close to our job. All the horror stories I had heard about people's pregnancies had me a bit afraid; but I had a great pregnancy. No nausea and I didn't even "show" that I was pregnant until I was almost six months along, which was great since I was new to my job. I was almost five months along before I told my supervisor and co-workers, and found them to be both supportive and wise. I was looking forward to everything happening just as scheduled. But my January 30th due date passed, and I felt as if I would be pregnant for the rest of my life. When my water broke on the evening of February 1, 1982, I was thrilled beyond measure.

Labor was not nearly as horrible as I had feared, and at 11:08 am on the morning of February 2, Jai Timothy Williams made his entrance into the world. He was born on Groundhog's Day, that famous day when a special groundhog named Punxatawny Phil is supposed to look for his shadow to predict the coming of Spring. I was so grateful that Jai didn't emerge from the womb, see his shadow and choose to go back inside. Weighing in at 6 pounds and 12 ounces and measuring 19 inches in length, Jai made me feel a love like I had never known. As I held my newborn son in my arms, my love quotient went through the roof. Being his mother made me feel so complete. We chose his name for two reasons. One, Tim had always signed his important documents, J. Timothy Williams. I was not about to ever name a child of mine "Jethro." Two, my best childhood friend spelled his name J-A-I. In my mind, there was no other possible way to spell that name. Tim was pleased beyond measure and, holding Jai for the first time, declared, "Better than my Baby and better than my Buddy, he's my Bubby!" To this day one of Jai's nicknames is "Bubby." Jai was my first known blood relative, and although I didn't know my history, I held my future with pride.

There are not enough words in the English language to describe how thrilled Mom and Daddy were to meet Jai for the first time. He was four days old when they arrived from Saginaw to dote on and spoil their new grandson. They came bearing gifts and food that rivaled the birth of a king. Grandparents' love is a special kind that knows no bounds and sees no flaws. In their eyes, Jai was perfect in every single way. And, naturally, I thought so, too.

As excited as we were to be parents, it took a while to get used to having a child. One evening when Jai was only 15 days old, Tim and I decided to take our new bundle of joy to prayer meeting. I wouldn't let anyone get their germs on him; but even though it was the dead of winter, I really wanted to get outside. We gathered all our baby equipment and headed out to the car, got in and began our 45-minute journey to the church. Conversation was light and happy as we rode down the highway when suddenly we both realized at the very same time that we had left Jai at home! We had to drive about a mile to reroute and head back home to find Jai, bundled in his snow suit, lying on the couch with sweat beads forming on his forehead. I'll never forget the expression on his face. Loosely translated, I think he was saying, "I have idiots for parents." That was the first of plenty of mistakes that I made with not only Jai but my other children as well. However, I don't think I left any of them ever again. I don't think I did. Did I? Well, I don't remember doing it ... at least not by accident.

Another thing that was hard to get used to was putting Jai in his car seat. When he was born, it was not yet the law for children to be in car seats. I grew up in a time where my mother's hand across my chest during a sudden stop was all the seatbelt I ever needed. When Jai was born, it was a huge debate as to whether children even needed such contraptions to hold them in place. But child car seats were all the rave, and Aunt Kathy and Uncle Don had insisted on purchasing a top-of-the-line model for Ruby's baby. I am eternally grateful to them for this wonderful and expensive gift of love.

I loved watching Bubby grow. Having never babysat or changed one diaper in my life before becoming a mother, I cherished every moment of care for my newborn son. It was vital to me that I nursed him, and I was fascinated at how fast he grew from the nourishment designed by God's own hand. We are, indeed, "fearfully and wonderfully made" (Psalm 139:14). It amazed me to watch him grow and change day by day. Little things that he couldn't do one day were completely mastered the next. As my child grew and developed, I was thrilled time and again at this gift called life. Jai fascinated me with every move, turn, yawn and grunt.

And how I enjoyed watching Tim with Jai. Fatherhood certainly agreed with him. My husband had not been pleased that I was pregnant so early into our marriage, and didn't offer much support during that tender time, so I wasn't sure exactly how he would be once our child was born. But he really surprised me. I don't believe I would have been able to hold my own baby, had I not been a nursing mother. Tim's demeanor softened tremendously and I was overcome with love. My home was where I loved to be. I stayed home nine months with my firstborn son and treasured every minute of it. When I returned to work, we chose a loving grandmotherly-type to watch over him in our absence. I did not know that a heart could be so filled with love. I thought I knew love before, but this I could neither explain nor deny. Grateful, ever so grateful for the gift of his life, I found myself in deeper communion with God and more closely connected to Tim.

One day when Jai was about six weeks old, Tim was tinkering with the sound system while Jai wiggled on the blanket beside him. "I'm teaching my son about electronics," he proudly announced. I laughed at the thought of Jai working on electronic equipment before he could crawl. Inadvertently the microphone passed in front of the speaker and gave an awful screech. Jai did not flinch. We both noticed it and were immediately deeply concerned. Was our child hearing impaired? I called to ask my mother, but Daddy answered instead. Upon hearing his voice, I began to cry.

"What's wrong, Baby?" he tenderly asked.

"I think Jai is deaf," I sobbed.

"What? Why?" he demanded.

As I explained what had just happened, Daddy's voice became stern. "There is nothing wrong with my grandson, ya hear? NOTHING! Now, your mother's not home, but when she gets here, she will call you. And she'll tell you the very same thing!" He quickly hung up the phone, leaving me staring at the receiver in my hand.

I told Tim what Daddy said, but then I got the phone book (this is before Google, remember?) and I looked up Columbus Speech and Hearing Center. The man with the understanding voice on the other end reassured me that six weeks was too young to identify hearing deficits at that time but if I were still concerned when Jai was three months old, I could schedule an appointment. He said the decibels would have to be about as loud as a vacuum cleaner before causing concern. His words made me feel a little better. But only just a little. I was convinced something was wrong with my child.

Mom called that evening and was a tad bit more reassuring than Daddy had been, but she, too, was quite confident that Jai was the most perfect being ever created by God. I wanted desperately to believe what she was saying, but my soul was telling me to pay attention.

Over the next year and some months, I would talk to our pediatrician, family physician and the Columbus Speech and Hearing Center again, and all seemed of the same opinion as Daddy. They made no bones about telling me that I was a neurotic, overly-sensitive, over-protective, first-time mother and had no cause for worry. During that time, I kept a loving and watchful eye on Jai's developmental progress. He walked at 10 months and began saying little words, "It's Jai!" when he saw himself in the mirror, "Me!" "Up" "Da-Da," which thrilled Tim beyond all measure, and "Mmmmm," which I declared was "Mom." He could identify body parts by pointing to them when we named them and loved to play, although not necessarily with other children. He had a healthy appetite, grew according to the charts, and mastered fine and gross motor skills.

From a very young age Jai was extremely regimented. He went to sleep and awakened as if on cue and kept his belongings and surroundings very neat and tidy. Mom was thrilled that her first grandson was so organized. He was meticulous about the arrangement of his toys. They had to turn a certain way and measure a precise distance between them. While most mothers complained of the messes their children made, I didn't have that worry at all. I especially recall a set of old keys Tim kept on a ring. Jai manipulated those keys off that ring and lined them up on a low shelf of the bookcase, each key in order and facing in the same direction. If we dared to moved one of those keys or even turn them in a different way, Jai would cry. We assumed that it was just his love for organization that caused him such pain.

Tim and I thought Jai to be brilliant, and he amazed us at his apparent maturity and well-behaved demeanor. Jai would sit for hours on end, playing with only one or two toys, barely making a sound. Other children were overly-active, almost destructive in nature, and could become quite loud at times, but Jai was calm, cool and collected, and always looked at those children as if they were crazy.

Both our pediatrician and family doctor said I was a new mother who was just overly concerned about nothing. My parents told me I was looking for trouble where there was none. My friends seemed to know of some family where some kid didn't talk until he was 30 and was a genius. But none of them could convince me that my concerns were unwarranted. In the back of my mind, I wondered if my apprehensions from that day when he was only six weeks old were legitimate. While I was not well versed in the development of young children, I knew that my son should be making more noise and be more active than he was at this stage in his life. My parents and husband seemed perfectly content with Jai, and while my love for him was deep and unwavering, I felt something was terribly wrong. I just didn't quite know what to do about it all.

When Jai turned 17 months old, I noticed that he was no longer adding new words to his vocabulary. Additionally, he seemed to be quickly losing the few words that he did know. Other children not quite as old were chattering and trying to communicate, but my son was sinking deeper and deeper into silence. We read to him daily, as we had done since before his birth, and we sang constantly as well as played all types of music in our home. But Jai spoke no words and hummed no tunes. By the age of 19 months, Jai could only say two words, "Be" and "Jai." Now Tim noticed what I had been referring to all along, and when I mentioned my need to call the Columbus Speech and Hearing Center again, he agreed that it was the right thing to do. This time when I explained my concerns, an appointment was scheduled immediately. I knew something was wrong and braced myself for the bad news.

The day of testing arrived quickly and within minutes of their evaluation, Tim and I were called into a room with three professionals. Although they introduced themselves, I cannot for the life of me remember who they were or what they did. But I remember, word for word, what was said to us. "Total hearing loss in his right ear ... and partial hearing loss in his left ear ... referring you to the Nisonger Center for follow up. Here is their number ... All I heard was "Blah ... blah ... blah ... blah – blah ... blah ... blah." When you are getting unfavorable news, sometimes the words sound garbled and it's difficult to comprehend what's really being said. Apparently, the testing revealed partial hearing loss in one ear and some deficit in the other, but they said that the tests were inconclusive.

"We just want to tell you our initial findings," the tall pale doctor spoke behind thick lenses. "We believe your son is autistic."

Smiles broadened across both Tim's and my face. "That's it!" Tim was the first to speak, as my face lit up the room. "Artistic. That makes sense!!" "Yes," I echoed his enthusiasm. "He loves to draw! It makes sense that he would be artistic!" Words poured out of our mouths like the famous Niagara Falls.

"No, Mr. and Mrs. Williams," the somber, plain-looking female doctor with severely chapped lips interrupted. "We believe your son is autistic, not artistic. AUTISTIC." She continued talking but I only heard an empty void.

A dead silence fell upon the room. Autistic? What in the world was THAT?

"Auto means self – we believe your son is disappearing inside of himself," a third unnamed doctor spoke to tell us that there wasn't a lot of information on autism, but basically children who had not been properly nurtured and loved by their mothers were more likely to end up with autism. "We believe that he will never talk and never get out of diapers. He will have to be institutionalized and you will never be able to raise him in your home... blah ... blah ... blah." This professional was telling us that my child was doomed to life as a low-level functioning human being.

I don't remember leaving the Columbus Speech and Hearing Center, getting in the car or heading home that day. Tim and I always had pleasant car conversations, but that day neither of us spoke, each of us deep in our own thoughts. I wanted to cry, scream, stomp, rant and rave, but instead I was totally silent. I felt autistic myself at that moment, completely disappearing inside of myself.

And with that, we were plunged into a world that was new, foreign and uncertain. The prognosis was dismal at best. We never discussed the professionals' comments. Neither of us had ever heard that word before in our lives. Imagine a time in earth's history when we had not heard of AIDS or the internet or yes, even autism. There were no organizations or puzzle-shaped pieces that represented this disorder. No special walks or colorful ribbons to pin on the lapel. In fact, my library search only uncovered a handful of books and one movie about the subject. I realized the "experts" didn't know what they were talking about. And they certainly didn't know Jai, me or my God. I knew something was wrong, but I also knew that it wasn't hopeless.

The "Gloom and Doom Team" referred us to the Nisonger Center, an early intervention specialty center connected with Ohio State University. Before we left the Hearing Center, they scheduled our appointment for October 15, 1984 at 9:00 am. But we never made it to that appointment.

Over the next few months, Tim and I weighed our options. We would learn American Sign Language to be able to fully communicate with Jai. We would treat him the same as we always had. He would need discipline, responsibilities and structure. And our son would need his mother full time if he were to have a successful life. Our plan was for me to eventually quit my job to focus my attention on getting Jai through this hurdle of his young life. During this time, perhaps we could have another child and I would concentrate on home while Jai and his sibling were young. Although I was ever so sad, Daddy's words returned to my heart to encourage me, "you either laugh or your cry. I choose to laugh." And might I add, I chose to dance. Besides, Jai knew how to imitate our facial expressions and seemed to pick up our moods, and I was determined to keep my attitude and disappointment in check. I wanted to be a positive influence in his life. It was important to me that I sang to Jai, read to him and talked with him as if he were conversing freely with me.

I began to use multiple descriptive words to explain simple actions. For example, I would say something like this: "I am going to make a sandwich with two slices of whole wheat bread," "And, using a butter knife from the left side of the kitchen drawer, I am going to spread white mayonnaise and yellow mustard on this brown bread. I will also add yellow cheese, red tomatoes, green lettuce and ... what color is this meat? Tan maybe? Okay. Tan meat it is!" Steps were counted, letters were pointed out on signs, colors were explained in detail. Sweet, sour, happy, sad ... I did everything I could to make Jai's world vibrant with words. During this season of his life, he never responded, or even acted as if he knew what I was saying, but I was determined he would be able to read, write, count and function in this world.

Jai's babysitter, Mrs. Ethel Atkinson, was wonderful as well. She spent extra time and care with Jai, showing him how to tend the vegetables in her small garden. Sometimes when we picked him up he would show us some small token from the garden, a tomato or green pepper, and his smile would light up the room. I could tell that he loved the outdoors. Working with the soil is a way to communicate with the Creator and I am ever grateful to the entire Atkinson family for how they cared for Jai. Mrs. Atkinson assured me that nothing would change the way she watched over Jai and that initial diagnosis meant nothing to her. "He's a little boy," she said emphatically. "And that's all that matters to me." Blessed. That's what we were.

September of 1984 I said good-bye to my wonderful work family at Chemical Abstracts Service. While I knew I would miss them, I was excited about my new adventure. My daily routine was great, and I was happy to be a full-time wife and mother. After five weeks of being home, Jai and I took a road trip to Michigan. Our plan was to visit with my parents for about a week or maybe two, to spend some quality time with Daddy. He had been diagnosed with liver and colon cancer and the doctors said he had about six months to live. Time with

Daddy would be precious indeed. Then we would visit Tim's sister, Darlene, who had just had her second child. I couldn't wait to meet my new niece.

We arrived in Saginaw on a Sunday. My parents were elated to see us, and I could tell that Daddy's spirits were lifted just by our walking through the door. For me it was a time to really get some much-needed rest. Mom would tend to Jai, cook delicious meals and the time with my family was sure to bring laughter and love. We were planning our week and I was excited to be able to see old friends, visit my home church and show them how much Jai had grown. I was sure to return home with new clothes for all of us; that was how my parents were.

But on Tuesday evening, Tim called and told me he missed me terribly. He wanted me to return home as soon as possible. *How rude!* I thought. I had just gotten to my parents' home and hadn't even gone to see HIS sister yet. I was not coming home, and that was final! We ended our conversation – I suppose I'm the one who ended it! But when I hung up the phone, my mother came and sat close to me on the couch.

"Ruth-Ann," she said directly, "when your husband calls and asks you to come home, you need to come home. He wouldn't ask if he didn't need you there. Now, me and your Dad will be all right. I'll help you get your things together." I didn't like what she said, but I somehow recognized the wisdom in her words. Without telling Tim, I set out for home on Wednesday morning. In hindsight, I am eternally grateful that I did.

When Tim drove down Brown Road in Grove City, around 4:30 pm on Wednesday, October 10, his wife and son were standing in the driveway waving. As he pulled in, he was grinning from ear to ear and there were tears in his eyes. He parked and exited the car, and hugged us tightly. He was glad we had returned home and apologized profusely for cutting our trip short. That evening he shared some things with me that explained why he needed me to return home; things that could not have been fully conveyed over the phone. But that evening I shared something with him as well – I was pretty sure I was pregnant again.

He turned to me with excitement and said, "Oh, you're pregnant! And it's gonna be a girl. And you are gonna name her Brittany Janae. She must have the initials BJ, since those are the only two words that Jai can say. Then he will always be able to say his sibling's name."

It struck me as strange that he said I would name her. We had always said that I would name the boys and he would name the girls. So, I asked, "Why am I gonna name her? Where are you gonna be?" He just smiled and said, "Ya never know."

CHAPTER TEN

Accidental Strength

Our weekend was filled with activity, and I was so grateful I had cut our trip short. Tim and I sang in a choir called "Oasis," and they had a concert on that Saturday night, which was well attended. Once Jai was born, I had taken a break from the group, but remained a huge supporter and fan. Under the direction of Dr. James Stewart, Oasis sang a variety of music from classical to gospel, and there would certainly be a song for everyone's tastes. One song that particularly touched me that night was "Do the Best You Can" and some of the lyrics were, "you may not be here tomorrow..." The woman who sang the lead part on that song stood directly in front of Tim, and while focusing on her solo, one couldn't help but see Tim smiling and singing behind her. That memory would remain in my mind for years.

After the concert, we went to Derrick and Robyn's house. The men watched the pre-recorded final World Series game, but the video recording ran out in the bottom of the ninth inning with bases loaded and two outs. Our beloved Detroit Tigers had won the World Series, but we didn't know that yet.

The women chatted and fussed over food in the kitchen and dining areas. Robyn and Derrick had just gotten a hot tub and we ladies were excited to try it out. But I hesitated to get in, and when Robyn asked me about it, I shared with her that I thought I might be pregnant and there had been stern warnings issued to expectant mothers about the dangers of sitting for prolonged periods of time in water hotter than body temperature. I wasn't going to take any chances, and instead sat on the edge and dangled my feet in the steaming tub. The next day we were to return to their home to help them clean out their garage, or was it the basement? It didn't really matter to me because I wasn't planning to do much of anything. I would just offer plenty of moral support. Normally I would have helped, at least a little bit, but since I was pretty sure I was pregnant again, I didn't want to overdo it, at least that's the excuse I would use. If it turned out that I was not pregnant, then I would have gotten to hang out with some wonderful people.

We were to arrive around noon, but for some reason, Tim went to work early that Sunday morning. When he returned home around 10:30, he was extremely excited that he had completed a two-year project in about six months' time. As a systems analyst, he had been given the huge task of updating the entire pay roll system for our company. CAS was going to now have direct deposit. It was his first major project and he had been given the lead portion to complete. The projected time for completion was two years, but he had worked tirelessly to complete this task early, which would certainly grant him a handsome raise and a huge promotion. He described all the details, mostly in a language that I barely understood. The bits and bytes of computer-lingo were way over my head. But I listened intently as Jai played quietly in the corner. Excitement was the watchword of the day. I was so happy for him and delighted in his accomplishments. This completion of this project, along with the finishing of his PhD, would open many doors of opportunity for him.

I wanted us to hurry up and get going. After all, our friends were expecting us to be there in a timely manner. But for some reason, Tim wanted to call his youngest sister, Darlene. He did not rush through that conversation, while I nervously tapped my foot and paced around the living room, wondering when he was going to get off that phone and come on so we could leave. Keep in mind that this was all before cell phones, so it's not as if Tim could just talk to her while we were on the road. After what felt like multiple delays, we were finally on our way. But instead of getting on the highway and taking our usual route, Tim chose to leisurely drive through the city, which seemed so very odd to me. We soon pulled up into the parking lot of an army supply store. At this point I had resigned myself to the fact that we were just gonna be late. Tim seemed anxious to show me something special. As I climbed out of my seat, Tim unbuckled Jai from his "Cadillac Car Seat" that top-of-the-line well-constructed, leather padded holder for our firstborn. How precious that gift soon became!

When we entered the store, I was fascinated by the variety of items. I found myself enjoying this storehouse of everything military. I tried to meander but Tim was focused on one specific item. Leading me to the back corner of the store, I saw what appeared to be a stack of pillows. Further investigation showed jeep seats, the removable seats that fit into military vehicles. My puzzled look was no match for his priceless facial expression as he excitedly told me the reason for the jeep seat. Tim wanted Jai to be able to transition out of his high chair because we were hoping to have another baby within the year. He did not want Bubby to feel forced out by the arrival of a sibling, so his plan was to teach Jai to sit directly at the table with the help of this 18-inch square, 9" thick, well-made and easy-to-clean seat. It could be safely tucked away when not in use. Once he explained its purpose, I was thrilled that we had taken this short detour and agreed with him that it would be a wise purchase for only $3.00.

Returning to the car, Tim opened the door and placed that jeep seat on my side and told me to sit on it. I giggled, climbed atop the newly-bought, repurposed jeep seat, and secured my seat belt. He carried Jai to the back and strapped him in. Two days before, he had moved his car seat from directly behind the driver to the middle seat so that Jai could see out of the front window as we drove. Those two final acts – placing the jeep seat on my side and shifting Jai to the middle seat – would save our lives. Tim hopped into the car and, reaching over to snap his seatbelt in place, he smiled the biggest smile and declared, "Finally, you're as tall as I am!" That comment made me laugh, since Tim stood a full ten inches above me.

Contentment combined with early pregnancy, and I quickly drifted off to sleep. It felt as if I had been asleep for hours when I was suddenly awakened by an extremely loud noise accompanied by a severe pain in my back. I was immediately nauseous and disoriented for a moment, and then I looked to my left. Tim's eyes were closed and his hands had fallen into his lap. But my eyes didn't linger there long at all. As a mother, my first concern was for Jai. I looked past Tim, only later registering what I observed, and when my eyes landed on Jai, I went into full panic mode. Jai's face had turned ashen gray and blood was pouring from his head. At that point, all the color went out of my world.

An unknown man came up to my side of the car and asked if I was okay. I insisted that I was, but I wanted him to get Jai out and give him to me. I needed to hold my son. And I kept saying repeatedly that I thought I might be pregnant. The pain in my back was so intense that I believed I could actually feel and hear blood running in my body. Everywhere I looked, I saw black and white and gray and I couldn't understand what was happening to me and Jai. The man quoted some First Aid mumbo-jumbo about not moving accident victims and I grabbed at his shirt, frantically insisting that he unfasten my child and give him to me. He hesitantly loosened Jai, lifted him from the back and placed him on my chest. The streaming blood from his opened head wound painted my white jacket a deep crimson, but I cared not at all about my clothes. Jai was limp and weak in my arms, unmoving and still. I was convinced he was dead and I didn't want to live anymore. I held onto my firstborn for dear life and found myself unable to speak or hear or think. By now more onlookers had stopped and paramedics had arrived. Everyone seemed focused on Tim, but I could not move. The pain in my back had localized on the left side, behind my heart, and any movement or breathing was excruciating. I finally inhaled slowly and turned my head to the left. Tim was very still, and I noticed a bit of drool escaping his mouth.

Next thing I knew, I was on a stretcher and being placed in an ambulance. They literally had to pry Jai out of my arms, and he was brought into the ambulance with me. In that moment, I was reduced to my most common denominator, as it were. The only thing that came into my spirit was the first song I had ever learned back in the church of Saginaw Michigan. I began to hum the tune, "Yes, Jesus loves me! Yes, Jesus loves me! Yes, Jesus loves me ..." and then, in the faintest, most beautiful sound I had ever heard, Jai completed the verse by humming, "... for the Bible tells me so!" In that instance, I had proof that my son, whom I was convinced had not survived the accident, was alive! And then the color returned to my world.

I heard my attending paramedic say to his driver, "No sirens. This one's hurt pretty badly," but my sense of humor was now able to kick in, and I said, "Turn on all the sirens and lights. I've never been in an ambulance before and I want everyone to know that I'm coming!"

Everyone who came my way heard my concern – I think I might be pregnant. The pain was so intense I was sure I would pass out soon, and I didn't want anything done to me that would possibly harm my unborn child.

Jai was dropped off at Children's Hospital before the ambulance took me to another place. By now I was in such discomfort that I never stopped to think that my child's first hospital experience would be without his parents.

There was no waiting when I arrived at Grant Hospital's emergency room. They whisked me back to the triage area for assessment and treatment. Initial tests confirmed that I was, indeed, pregnant. Doctors told me the X-rays showed five broken ribs, although my films now show it was actually six that were broken. An angiogram revealed my heart was strong, but the broken portion of one of those ribs was dangerously close to my aorta. One false move, an aggressive hug or even a violent sneeze could cause the sharp edge of the broken rib to nick my aorta, resulting in instant death. My physicians wanted me in intensive care on high doses of pain medications, but I refused to take anything stronger than Tylenol.

Months before the accident, Robyn and I had made a pact – should anything happen of an emergent nature, we would be each other's sister. She's also a nurse, which helped her to gain entrance into my intensive care Room 309. It was wonderful to see her and she did the acting job of a Grammy Award winning actress during her first hours with me, for she was guarding a secret that was not to be revealed to me until my parents' arrival. Tim was in grave condition and was not going to live. Mom and Daddy arrived late that night and were crying uncontrollably. Not understanding the gravity of the situation, I kept trying to reassure them that I would be all right. I told them where Jai was and that Tim had been taken to Doctor's North Hospital. I asked them to go to our home, gather a few items along with our wedding picture to take to Tim's bedside. I implored them to please tell him that I was pregnant with our second child. "Let him know that I am all right, Jai will be fine, and I'll see him soon." Mom ran out of the room several times muffling sobs and Daddy couldn't get himself together at all. I had no idea how tragically my road had turned.

The next morning, our family doctor walked into Intensive Care Room 309 with my parents shuffling close behind him. Neither of them looked at me as he offered the news in a callous and matter-of-fact way.

"Good morning, Ruth-Ann," his tone was flat and uncaring. "Timothy has passed away. We need your signature to remove him from the life support system."

My mind kicked into gear immediately and I somberly said, "Wow. I'm a widow at 24. Can we donate his organs?"

The stoic doctor seemed surprised by my request and he stuttered his answer, "Why y-y-y-yes, we can. I'll get the paperwork."

He exited and returned quickly, neither me nor my parents speaking in his absence. I signed the paperwork in red ink, *Ruth-Ann Williams... I love you, Tim.* Then I thought to ask, "Can you keep him alive until his mother gets here?" Someone had told me that they were en route from South Carolina. I later found out that, at their own expense, two wonderful pastors, Calvin Preston and Marcellus Howard, had driven my in-laws up to Columbus. Those caring souls made certain that Mama and Dad didn't have to make the almost-eight-hour journey alone.

The doctor assured me that they would sustain Tim until his parents' arrival. Emanuel and Naomi Williams arrived in Columbus late afternoon on Monday. Tuesday morning Tim was taken into surgery, his organs were harvested and his death was pronounced at 10:00 a.m. I'm told that he gave a new start to seven people that day. Two were given sight, two were taken off dialysis, two were able to breathe on their own and one was given a liver transplant. However, my request to keep him sustained until his parents' arrival caused them to use extraordinary measures that made his heart unusable.

It all happened so fast. One minute we were on our way to our friends' house for an afternoon of fun. The next minute I was a widow and the course of my life has remained forever changed. Jai was discharged from the hospital and Mrs. Atkinson took him home with her. I walked out of intensive care the next day against medical advice to be with my son and provide as much stability as possible. Elder Henry M. Wright, the president of our conference, escorted me home. He had left a major meeting in Washington, D.C. to check on me. Elder Wright was one of Tim's mentors, had given us pre-marital counseling, and offered spiritual blessings upon Jai when he was born. He would go on to bless my other two sons as well. Having him by my side was a gift of immeasurable worth.

After leaving the hospital, my first stop was to the Atkinson's home to pick up my son. When Jai looked up and saw me, we grabbed each other and held on for dear life. Still unsure of how much he could grasp, I found a quiet area and had him climb up beside me on the seat. "I love you, Bubby," I began, holding back tears that eventually spilled from my eyes. "And Daddy loves you too. I want to tell you something. The accident that hurt you and Mommy also hurt Daddy very badly. Daddy is dead. He's not going to be with us anymore." Jai had been looking deeply into my eyes, and upon hearing the dreadful news, held on to me as if I were his only life raft, and let out the most gut-wrenching, pitiful wail I've ever heard. We sat there for quite a while, the only sounds were our collective cries. My parents and Aunt Ella observed the tender scene. In that moment, I knew that Jai understood. Grief ran deeper than autism.

Support for our family came from everywhere. Church members, neighbors, co-workers and friends poured into our tiny starter home with food, flowers, monetary gifts, prayers and encouraging words. My friends Tina, Gwen and Margie came to support me – Tina and Margie were newly married and I had been matron-of-honor at both of their weddings. Tara's firstborn son had arrived on the 15th, so she was certainly in no condition to travel, but we spoke often during that time. I am eternally grateful to those who tended to our family's needs under such impossible circumstances.

My parents and Tim's parents and siblings were drenched in grief and we were no real help or support for each other. I am ever grateful for Allan and Shirley Cody Johnston, friends from Nashville. Shirley and Tim were raised together in Buffalo. With full knowledge of the situation, they flanked me on either side and guarded my broken ribs. I believe people could have gotten into Fort Knox easier than touching me during Tim's wake and funeral. Shirley didn't care if you were the highest-ranking official of the world, she wouldn't let you get near me! I am convinced that her watchcare over me saved my life. After the funeral, Tina and Margie stayed with me for a week. Their organizational skills and culinary delights ministered to me and Jai's needs and their presence and love helped me adjust to young widowhood.

During that time of incredible loss and excruciating physical pain, I found every opportunity to smile, and tried to keep things as normal as possible for Jai. His injuries were much milder than Tim's and mine, thank the Good Lord and that top-of-the-line-car seat from Aunt Kathy and Uncle Don. He had a concussion, a black eye and slight facial paralysis that would heal in time. It was vital to me that I held on to a positive outlook for the sake of Jai and my unborn child. It was vital that I found a way to dance, to believe that we would all survive this ordeal. That was a tall order to fill.

Assessing me after the accident, Dr. Bryan offered his professional recommendation that I abort my baby. "You've been through too much and the fetus is probably not going to be viable. All of the x-rays and the angiogram probably harmed the embryo." I refused. "You already have a special needs child. How will you handle two children without the support of your husband?" I refused. He told me, "Ruth-Ann, I cannot be your doctor if you continue with this pregnancy," to which I responded, "Doc, I've already had a child. I know that I do most of the work in labor. If you won't be my doctor, I'm sure I'll be okay."

Then he said, "Let me at least perform an amniocentesis." He assured me there was only a five percent chance of miscarriage with this relatively new procedure. But when I found out that involved placing a needle into my uterus, I refused that as well. "My unborn child has had enough trauma. I will not introduce anything else to it." I was emphatic. Finally, the doctor came around to my way of thinking – well, sort of. He said he would deliver, but he wanted the child born at Ohio State University Hospital, which at the time was better equipped to handle neonatal challenges. I agreed, and he offered a sigh of relief.

The prognosis had not been favorable for my father. In October of 1983, almost exactly a year before Tim's death, the doctors had found something suspicious that turned out to be cancer. By the time it was discovered, it had already spread from his colon to his liver and beyond and his oncologist told us he had about a year to live. He immediately signed up for an experimental drug/research program through the University of Michigan, at the age of 69. His mother had died from breast cancer and his other brothers had each succumbed to some form of cancer as well. He believed that enough was enough, and was hoping to do his part to help the medical community cure this disease. He was very sick at the time of Tim's death and we all knew that Daddy didn't have much time left on this earth. I was praying that he would live long enough to see my and Tim's last child born.

Although my due date was June 19, my father kept prophesying that "this baby will be born on Father's Day," which was scheduled to be June 16th that year. "That's the only gift I want on that day." How I wanted that to happen for Daddy, but of course, I had absolutely no control over that whatsoever. Yet I still prayed consistently that Daddy's request would be granted.

My pregnancy was excruciatingly painful. Ribcages are designed to expand as they accommodate the growing baby, and every expansion hurt me terribly. I was informed that the broken ribs would not even begin to heal until the child was delivered and I had completed nursing, nature would insure the baby's needs came first. I refused to take anything for pain because I wanted to give "Baby BJ" every possible advantage to arrive into this world safe and whole. Tending to Jai was easy and that helped a lot.

During my pregnancy another friend, Belinda, also a nurse who was pregnant with her first son, spent some time with me too. She was always ready with a quick wit and our time together was meaningful and good for my soul. I pray it was good for hers too. And my trio-singing buddy, Renee visited, bringing sunshine, prayers and wonderful walks down memory lane. Those visits along with the consistent calls and visits helped the time pass quickly. A group of men from my church volunteered to paint the nursery and assemble the crib for me. Neighbor and friend Vanessa painted a beautiful mural above the crib. She and hubby, Tom, helped with yardwork and simple household repairs. I had a great team of friendship and love that helped me survive this difficult time. There aren't enough words of gratitude to express my genuine appreciation.

The Saturday night before Father's Day, I was pleasantly surprised when my water broke. I was at home. Mom and my friend and birthing coach, Linda, were there and we all waited in rapt anticipation until my body showed the signs that labor was progressing. At this rate, the child would be born on the date Daddy had predicted. June 16, 1985, at 11:48 a.m., Brandon Je'Zhon

Williams made his entry into this world, weighing in at seven pounds and a quarter ounce. My doctor cried harder than I did at this perfect child. "Every now and then," he declared, "medicine has to bow to an Almighty God!"

How bittersweet was his birth! Because he was born on Father's Day, there was a special steak dinner prepared by the hospital for new parents. Special flowers were sent to me with a matching boutonniere for my husband – because he was born on Father's Day. With each shift change, I had to explain that my husband was dead and we wouldn't be celebrating anything together ever again. I finally called for the head nurse and when she arrived I asked her to please put a black band around my door, or whatever she had to do to stop the constant barrage of Father's Day greetings. These outbursts of joy and exclamation were just too much for me to bear. I don't know what she did, but I was not invited to another celebration for the remainder of my stay.

Brandon's birth announcement had a picture of Tim and I on the front. It was a double exposed picture that we had taken of each other while we were dating. The inside read: Tim's last and most precious gift to me and Jai was born on Father's Day …

From his first day on this earth Brandon seemed to absorb knowledge like a sponge. He studied his surroundings and calculated his moves carefully and deliberately. As he grew, he would constantly challenge me to be better, think deeper and question everything. When Brandon was four weeks old, Mom called to tell me that it was time to come home. I stuffed dirty clothes into pillow cases, buckled up my two sons and headed north for what would be my last moments with Daddy. Not knowing what to expect, I was surprised to see him looking so well. It seemed as if the doctors had been mistaken. He was anxious to see his grandson, but was too weak to hold him. He asked me to lay him on his chest. Kissing the top of Brandon's head, he cried genuine tears of gratitude. "Thank you," he whispered. "Thank you for my Father's Day gift."

For the baby's 2:00 a.m. feedings, I would go into Daddy's room and sit with him. He wasn't sleeping well now and those moments were precious. Early one morning Daddy asked, "What day is it?" When I answered him, he simply said, "February 28, 1914 to July 31, 1985." Within hours, eight days after my arrival, Daddy closed his eyes in death, surrounded by the love of family. A great man left a great legacy and is terribly missed to this very day.

I was five weeks pregnant when my husband died. That baby was five weeks old when my father died. Reggae international icon Bob Marley said it best: "You never know how strong you are until being strong is your only choice."

CHAPTER ELEVEN

Deep Valley: Sweet Fruit

It had been so exciting to watch our first house being built from the ground up, and though it was a small starter home, it held precious memories. I was advised not to make any major moves for at least a year after the accident. Since I, too, was injured in that accident, and had a baby on the way, moving was hardly high on my list of priorities. The more time passed, and especially once Brandon was born, the more my life became unbearable. I found myself overwhelmed with the cares of my life, stressed about the responsibility of an uncertain future with a special needs child, and unsure about my now one-year-old son's future without his father's guidance. At bedtime, I'd wonder if I'd ever make it through the night, then wake up and wonder if I'd make it through the day. I stood at my kitchen sink one day, not wanting to live anymore.

There are those who will say that I was experiencing a lack of faith in God or that I was faltering in my Christian journey. To them I will simply say that you have no idea how I was feeling at the time. Depression can weigh you down like a 50-pound bowling ball wrapped around each foot and if you are not careful, it will begin a seductive dance that woos you to end it all. At first, I took halted steps, most unsure of the proper movements and unconvinced that I wanted to travel down this road. The haunting tune that Depression hummed in my ear caused my body to melt into the lull and my body slowly began to rock to its rhythm. The more I listened to the mesmerizing tune, the more I was convinced that Death held my only answer and offered my only hope. I continued to sway back and forth, back and forth until my heart matched its choreographed steps – and I twirled and leaped, convinced that death was the only way to assure that I would be in control of my own future. I wasn't turning my back on God. Rather, I truly believed at that time that I was advancing closer toward Him, that this was His solution to my problem, and after death I would soon be engulfed fully in His loving embrace. My sons' futures looked bleak to me as well and I had decided to take them with me into eternity's welcoming arms.

I became enamored with the thought of just not being here. Those closest to me had no clue what I was planning to do to my children and myself. My routine was that every Thursday I would go out and find something new to wear for me and my sons. Then I would grocery shop. On Friday, I would clean my house, cook elaborate meals and prepare for church the next day. After church, I would invite people home with me, we would enjoy their wonderful company, and sometimes they'd even stay late into the evening. But Sunday through Thursday I would take to my bed, having very little contact with anyone and would dream of ending our lives. I had set the date, the time, the details. I had decided that it would take a while for people to miss us, and by then it would be too late. And since I am an organizer, I had our final days planned out perfectly. I no longer wanted to live. I didn't want anyone to stop me, and I would be sure to offer no warning or subtle signs.

The Sunday before my plot was to be executed, I was standing at the kitchen sink when again my world turned black and white. Feeling overwhelmed, exhausted and downright lonely, everywhere I looked, I only saw black and white and gray. My mind went back to the times as a child when my childhood friend, Jai and I played jacks. I remembered trying to hold all the jacks, as it were, in my hand. All the responsibilities, all the uncertainty, all the pain and grief, all the children. It was all too much. I wondered if I would have the courage to do what I had convinced myself must be done – I sincerely believed I needed to end it all. My future was dismal, my days bore no sunshine, and my world was void of color. That night I prayed what I determined would be my final talk with God on this earth. It was short. To the point. No flowery "Thee's" and "Thou's" – "God. I can't do this anymore. If You are real, stop me." I did not even have the strength to offer an "Amen."

Sleep has always come easily for me – a blessed gift from God. When I woke the next morning, still seeing everything in black and white, I got Jai up, dressed and on his bus. Then with the baby and me still in our pajamas, I got us in the car and headed to Jai's school. When we arrived at The Childhood League Center, I unfastened Brandon from the car seat and half dragged him into the school with me. I remember letting him down to run, but I have no idea where he went. I walked straight into the school counselor, Peggy's office and took a huge chance. Without asking if this was a good time or even acknowledging that she may have had other things to do, I blurted out my deadly plan and divulged every single detail. If she was horrified, she never showed it. If she needed a break from my non-stop barrage of pain, she never let on. If she was offended by my silken pink pajamas and fluffy house shoes, she gave no hint. She just listened. Tenderly and attentively, she listened. And she also came up with a perfect plan for me and my children. After one phone call, she had secured a foster home for my sons. My assignment was to go home, with Brandon, and pack two weeks' worth of clothes. Then, once Jai returned home from school, I was to take the boys to a house in Worthington. On the next morning, I was to go to Harding Hospital, a psychiatric facility, and check myself in. Had that happened today, she would have been required to take my children immediately and it would have taken months or perhaps even years to get them returned to me. I left that school with more hope than I had felt in a very long time.

Grateful to feel heard and understood, and actually relieved that I would still be alive, I went home and tended to Brandon as best I could. My vision was altered and yet I had the daunting task of packing their clothing. I just couldn't do it. Grabbing all the clothes out of all their dresser drawers, I dumped them all into the middle of the living room floor. And then I panicked. I needed to talk to someone, but who could I speak with about this situation? Normally, I would have called my mother, but Mom was in denial about my even having issues and trying to function. She felt that everything would be okay and I was never to act like anything was wrong or that I had trouble managing my life. Throughout the months after losing Tim and Daddy, whenever I'd try to talk with her about how sad I was and how much I was struggling, she would just brush it off. Mom's answer to everything was to just keep moving forward as if nothing had ever happened. "Visine your eyes," she'd say, which meant to never let anyone know you've been crying. That may have work for her, but it did not work for me.

I had the mental strength for one call and one call only. Remembering that my dear friend, Tara, had just had her second child, I took a chance and called her number. This was before cell phones, so it was difficult to get in touch with people unless they were home. She answered on the second ring! I immediately began to apologize for calling her, knowing she was tending to a brand-new baby, but I desperately needed her help. Hurriedly explaining my plight, I asked her to help me pack the boys' clothes. She lived six hours away from me! It was challenging to match colors because everything looked black and white to me. But she patiently walked me through the packing process, then continued to talk to me for several hours. My phone bill charge for that one call was over $500, but it was well worth the investment. She literally saved my life. Additionally, she somehow got word to a mutual friend, Allan, who drove six hours from Nashville to Grove City and accompanied me when I took the boys to their foster parents' home. When we pulled up to that house in Worthington, Ohio, I felt the color returning to my world.

I could not find that house again today if my life depended upon it, but back then, when my very life and the lives of my sons depended upon it, that house was a beacon in the night. The family was kind, as I recall, and the boys entered without fear. To those who offer the proper respite care to families such as mine, I owe you a debt of gratitude. You cared for my babies when I was in such crisis. Great foster homes are a blessing and are put in place for those who need it most. When I picked up Jai and Brandon two weeks later, they were happy and healthy. I am still so grateful to that family for being there, to Peggy, the kind social worker, who heard my heart and found my children shelter, and to God above for His tender mercies toward me. Because of yet another social worker, my family was made whole. And, of course, I am grateful to Tara.

If any one of those things had not been in place, I know I wouldn't be here to tell this story. The school counselor. The waiting foster family. Tara. Allan. The wonderful team at Harding Hospital. But God had worked out every detail and paved every road that led to His sustaining power. I think of the lives I would have missed, the moments I'd have not seen, the places I'd have not visited had my life ended that day. And yet I have complete compassion for that Ruth-Ann; I embrace her and love her continually, with understanding and profound love. She was strong and brave; fearless in the face of indescribable pain and extreme sadness and loss. She is still my hero.

I had no life plan, for I assumed it would all be over. Now the real work began. During the two weeks the boys were in foster care, I entered an intensive counseling program, new and innovative at that time, where I was in one-on-one care for six hours per day. My out-of-therapy assignment was to rest, eat well and journal. I had to "talk" about loss and pain and deal with the good and bad, ups and downs of my until-then life. I had failed to make the connection that my adoption, portions of my home life and marriage, along with the deaths of my close friend, husband and father, had affected me profoundly. I thought that as a Christian, I was showing signs of weakness and disbelief if I dared to admit that I was hurting inside. I was raised to smile no matter what, and to continue to be positive even in the face of great sorrow. Through counseling I could recognize and break through many of the myths that had governed my life. The work was arduous and tedious. Had I not committed to doing the required work, I would have had to go into in-patient treatment for a minimum of six weeks. I did not want to be away from my sons for that long!

Because I sleep so soundly, I had been forcing myself to stay awake until after 1:00 am, the time that Brandon awakened in the middle of the night. Although it was just for a few minutes, he would call out for me, and if I were sleeping, I would not hear him. I needed rest.

Because I was the only living parent, all medical and educational decisions had to be handled by me. Even well-baby care appointments and the simple, good things of life, all fell upon my shoulders. Grocery shopping, car repairs, yard work, birthday parties, tummy aches, swimming lessons – whatever it was, it all fell on me. I needed a plan.

Even though I was constantly making sure the boys were being properly fed and had their regularly scheduled meals, I wasn't eating properly. I needed nutrition.

Because there weren't many people to talk with about my multiple losses, I was overcome with grief. I needed counseling.

Because so many irons were in the fire, so many plates were spinning in the air – or whatever phrases are used to explain having a lot of things going on at the same time – I was overwhelmed. I needed an outlet.

I desperately needed balance. To this day I've learned to adopt the HALT System:

H = Hungry
A = Angry
L = Lonely
T = Tired

I am careful to make sure that I never allow myself to get too Hungry, too Angry, too Lonely or too Tired. I learned that in one of my many group sessions, and I have found it to be a great barometer for myself. Whenever any of these four areas are out of balance, I suffer. It can be tough, especially for women, to maintain balance. But when we can manage well, it helps us tremendously.

When Jai and Brandon returned home, they were now able to live with a mother who was healing. As I continued to feed my own soul emotionally, physically and spiritually, our home was restored to order. For the first time in months, I returned to my joyful habit of rising early in the morning for personal Bible study and prayer. We began to have worship in the home again, which included singing vibrant songs with lots of motions to make them come alive for my sons. We instituted story time again, outdoor time and enjoyable meal times. And we danced! I no longer looked at Jai as someone who would never speak, but as a sponge that was soaking up all the knowledge his little mind could hold. I no longer looked at Brandon as approaching the "Terrible Two's" but as a child with a zest for life who possessed deep intelligence. I realized that I was not raising boys, but rather little people who would grow up one day to become men. I expected that they would become viable members of society. My depression almost cut that short, for all of us. My inability to appreciate all the hues of emotion that God has given and embrace all the seasons of life had almost cost my entire family our lives.

I thank God for that horrible chapter in my life. It gave me pause, showed me where to go for true healing and granted me understanding for others who battle with depression. It caused me to identify that look in other young women and mothers and to be able to encourage them along their walk. I now can offer not just prayer, but support, guidance and relationship building. Once relationships are forged, I find opportunities to openly and honestly share my story and, if warranted, will tenderly suggest the need for professional counseling. If a person had a diagnosis of diabetes, the Christian community would never tell them to just pray. Prayer would be just one of the tools, along with seeking proper medical advice, making dietary changes and soliciting the support of family and friends. But when someone is dealing with depression, we are quick to tell them to just pray and trust in God. Much more is needed. And I thank God for His guiding hand, giving me courage to speak up and ask for help. Talk about a life-saver!

In the Christmas season of 1986, my neighbors, Tom and Vanessa Carpenter, dropped by one evening to check on me. Their children were the same ages as Jai and Brandon, and they wondered why I had not decorated for Christmas this year. We had been doing so much emotional work, I didn't have the strength or desire to put up decorations. Besides, Brandon was just a year and a half, and I didn't think it would matter much to Jai. "Nonsense!" Tom declared and with that they were out of the house. Oh, well, I shrugged to myself.

Less than 30 minutes later, Tom and Vanessa returned with a Christmas tree, lights, gifts for the boys, cookies and all the delights of Christmas. They worked like Santa's helpers on turbo power, and before I could say "Jingle Bells" my home had been transformed into a winter wonderland! The television was on and suddenly we noticed that Jai was repeating every letter and word on the Wheel of Fortune game show. We stopped and listened some more and I believe we all had tears as we heard his little voice! Thank you, "Clark and Vanna," for making our Christmas so memorable that year! As an adult, Jai puts up Christmas decorations the day after Thanksgiving. It's his favorite time of year.

Summer of 1987 on Brandon's second birthday, we moved from Grove City to Gahanna. I often joked that I bought Brandon a house for his birthday! By now I was feeling so much better and my children were thriving. Jai was saying words, although still not talking in full sentences. He was doing well at The Childhood League Center. Brandon was a non-stop chatter box and could read his little books with ease. They were both growing so nicely and I was settling into life with my two boys.

It was during this time that I developed a friendship with Leonette. Her son, Anton, was Brandon's age and they played tirelessly together for hours. He couldn't say my name and called me "Aunt "Ruban," which delighted me to no end. Brandon was also friends with two of Robyn's sons, Gentry and Gregory. He had a more active social life than I did, but his outgoing personality brought many families into our lives. We were thriving. My newfound friends had no idea what I had survived.

My outlook and perspective completely changed. I no longer looked at myself as damaged. I had lost some excess weight, began to shop for flattering outfits and was getting my hair and nails done on a regular basis. I was feeling great about myself and the progress that I had so carefully made. One day I met a man I had only spoken to on the phone. He was a meeting planner who had helped me arrange trips for the youth of my church, and from that initial contact, we had managed to keep in touch and talk periodically. He was in town for a funeral at our church and one of the members introduced us. I immediately recognized the name and realized we had been talking all this time. Tall and handsome, we spent considerable time together, enjoying great conversation and wonderful laughs. It only takes one time to conceive a child, as I found out very quickly. When I told him I was pregnant, he told me he was married. Determined not to cause problems for him and his wife (they lived in another state) I kept his identity secret and went about the task of telling my family and friends that I was going to have another child. But I explained to him that I didn't want to cause his wife any pain, but I would never lie to my children and family about my baby's paternity.

I dreaded telling my mother. She had preached the importance of children being conceived inside of marriage, and I was expecting her to hit the proverbial roof. Instead, she asked me one question: "Are you going to have the baby?" I assured her that I was happy and planned to keep my child. Mom was thrilled. Another grandchild on the way! She was extremely supportive. Thankfully the pregnancy was easy and carefree.

Monday morning, September 12, 1988 was a beautiful sunny day and my friend, Lauretta, drove me to my doctor's appointment. Dr. Bryan thought I might be in labor, but had me walk around for an hour and return to his office. Sure enough, it was time for my child to enter this world, and the sunny day matched Austin Lamar's personality. He made his appearance at 5:45 pm. My biggest baby, he weighed eight pounds even, and I was in love from the moment I saw him. Austin had small, light-colored wisps of hair that made him look bald and my cousin Elaine said that he looked like he had a scoop of ice cream on top of his head. "I'll call him Scoopy," she said, which upset me to no end. "Don't call my baby, Scoopy! I won't have it!" I cried! But by the time he was three weeks old, I found myself calling him Scoopy! That's his nickname to this day, although he has shortened it to Scoop!

Austin has added much depth and many wonderful layers to my life. Always full of laughter and pranks, I am convinced Austin gave Jai the impetus to speak and Brandon the determination to prosper. He is my non-traditional child who always saw life through rose-colored glasses and despised traditional concepts. Mom was thrilled to have another grandson and considered him to be her personal birthday gift, since her birthday was four days later.

Life as a full-fledged member of the three-boys' club was extremely busy. There were days when I literally dropped into bed, completely exhausted. But I was ever so grateful for my children and felt my life was complete.

When Austin was three weeks old, his father met him and then brought his own mother to meet me and her newest grandchild. She held him with such tenderness and love, oohing and aahing over how much he looked like her son. Not a hint of condemnation did she show. The older brothers were napping when our visitors arrived, but as soon as they awakened, they bolted down the stairs. When the grandmother saw Jai, she recognized him immediately and let out a gasp. During her night shift as an RN at Children's Hospital, she had tended to the little boy whose father died in a horrible car accident and mother was in intensive care. She had wondered whatever became of that family and how Jai was doing now. When Jai saw her, I watched this child, who normally shrank from human touch, run to her, bury his head in her chest and laugh gleefully. Austin's grandmother had lovingly ministered to his big brother long before he was even born. She was a kind woman; always loving and caring towards Austin. She would spend quality time with him for many years.

In the Spring of 1989, Tina encouraged me to enroll in the Academy of Court Reporting. She was a court reporter and felt it would be a good career path for me to pursue. After researching the curriculum, I agreed with her. Austin was nine months old and just starting to crawl. Learning the keyboard of that odd-shaped machine was exciting and new. I was happy to be in school again and spent hours upon hours practicing for what would be my new vocation. People often ask me why there are no letters on the machine, and I remind them that there are no letters on piano keys either. The machine combines letters to make not only words, but also symbols and numbers. To graduate from court reporting school, I had to be able to "write" at the speed of 225 words per minute with 95% accuracy or above. Anything less was an "F". In conversational writing, we had to identify the speaker before they spoke and get every single word they said, even the "uh-huh's" and "uh-uh's." School proved to be a long and uphill journey and extremely challenging for me, but I was determined to finish. There were 17 students that started school with me. I am the only one from my class to graduate.

When Austin was 18 months old, I married Alvin S. Mosby in April of 1990. We had a huge wedding, and all my "girls" were there with me – Tina, Robyn, Leonette, Lauretta, Patty, Vanessa, Sheri, and my cousin Elaine. They still tease me about those "Smurf blue dresses" they had to wear, but it was a huge celebration with well over 500 guests in attendance. The boys and I relocated to Pittsburgh, Pennsylvania. Alvin and I began dating soon after Austin's birth and many people assumed that Austin was Alvin's child. He and I had met a few years earlier when I visited his city. We had spent long hours talking, sharing, visiting, and laughing, and the boys enjoyed having a man around. Before long, he had met my mom and extended family and I had met his family. Al was a hard-working, dedicated man with strong church ties. He was an excellent cook and I was amazed at his culinary delights. After he asked me to marry him, we spent time in counseling and were anxious to start our new life together. I would continue my court reporting education at Duff's Business Institute in Pittsburgh.

We chose to have a big wedding because this was Alvin's first marriage, and all our support systems were in attendance. We found what I considered to be my dream house and moved in there one month after marriage. Alvin's family is huge and I love them all. This was the first time I got to see all the hues and intricacies of family dynamics, and at times I was completely overwhelmed by this big family.

Living in this new state afforded me multiple opportunities for growth and change. For the first time in my life, I rode on public transportation, ate new and exciting foods and learned the "Pittsburghese" language. I met fascinating people and learned to maneuver the steep and continuous mountains of the Allegheny countryside. "There are seven ways down a mountain," Uncle "Gip" informed me. "Learn all seven of them, and you will be fine." My new church family, comprised of mostly Alvin's family, accepted me with open arms and I found myself settling into this new season of my life. Alvin's aunts and uncles became mine and I treasured the interactions I had with them all. There was a wealth of wisdom, and I soaked up their knowledge like a sponge, each one adding a new dimension to my life. The boys made lifetime friends and became men in Pittsburgh, Pennsylvania.

In the early morning hours of August 6, 1990, I received a phone call from my mother. As soon as I heard her voice, I knew something was terribly wrong. She sounded different, scared perhaps, and a little disoriented. She began the conversation by insisting that she was "all right", but I knew that she wasn't. Something had happened in the wee hours of the night and she never fully recovered from it for the remainder of her time on this earth. I listened intently as she shared this horrifying experience with me.

"I was extremely tired from working at the church in our evangelistic series," she began. "I got home late, took a shower and fell fast asleep around 10:30 pm. I was awakened by a sound, and then I immediately heard a hard shower of rain and thought maybe that's what I heard. But as I tried to settle back to sleep, I heard someone outside the kitchen window. It sounded like they were trying to break in. I called 9-1-1." My heart began to pound wildly inside my chest as I switched the phone's receiver to the other ear.

"The operator answered and I told her that I thought I heard someone trying to break in to my house and she asked me, 'Well, do you know who it is?' I told her, 'If I knew who it was, I would greet them at the door in a sexy black negligee; but I certainly wouldn't be calling YOU!' Then the lady told me, 'Well, unless someone is in your home, there is nothing we can do." And she hung up the phone!"

I sank onto the edge of the bed, incredulous! I couldn't believe that a trained operator had responded that way to my mother! She was a great citizen and had never called the emergency line before, so I just couldn't imagine why they would treat a senior citizen like that!

She continued her story as I gripped the receiver with both hands. "I thought maybe I hadn't heard what I knew I had heard. So, I tried to settle back down to get more rest. But then -- you know how I always prop a chair up between the back door and basement door for extra reinforcement?"

"Yeah," I answered. Mom had always been overly cautious about making sure all doors were locked and barricaded.

"Well," she said, "I heard that chair fall down the stairs!"

I gasped! "What did you do?"

"I called 9-1-1 AGAIN! This time I got a different operator, but was basically told the same thing; that unless I had proof that someone was in my house, there was nothing that they could do. I asked if they would just send a cruiser by to make sure everything was all right, but the lady told me they couldn't do that either."

"Oh no! Mom, what happened next?" I had now stood up and was pacing the bedroom floor, listening intently.

"Well, I got my gun," she stated matter-of-factly. "And grabbed my robe. And I sat on my bed and waited."

My heart was racing so quickly and pounding so loudly that I thought for sure Mom could hear it through the telephone lines! All I could manage to say was, "Oh, no!"

"By now I could hear that someone was actually in the house! I could hear the floorboards creaking in the kitchen and I could sense every movement that he was making. I thought he would just grab my VCR and TV, or maybe the radio in the kitchen. But he slowly maneuvered past all of those things and was heading directly toward my bedroom." Mom lived in a ranch-style home.

I felt paralyzed and as if every ounce of fluid in my body was frozen stiff. I had to force myself to breathe slowly and then Mom heard me gasp again.

"He was holding a little light, and I aimed the gun around where I imagined his body to be, in reference to the light. And then I shot the gun. I heard him drop to the floor, but I thought he was trying to fake me out."

I had now moved to my closet and began throwing clothes into a suitcase. My mother needed me and I would make the six-hour journey to Saginaw as soon as our conversation was over. "So, I shot the gun again. And this time he ran through everything that he had so carefully maneuvered around to get into the house. And he was screaming."

"Oh my God! What did you do next?" My voice loud and piercing. I was almost through with my packing.

"Well, he ran out the back door and I ran out the front. I went to our neighbors and started banging on their door. I still had the gun in my hand. When Mr. Screws opened the door, he must have wondered what had gotten in to me!" Mom was always able to find humor in every situation, and it was a small relief to hear her let out a quick laugh.

She continued with her story. "The next call to 9-1-1 was that someone had been shot!" Then she explained what happened when the police came, how they took her to the hospital, as she was so extremely shaken up. She called my Aunt Ella who was there quickly to tend to her. Aunt Ella has always been a slow and cautious driver. "Ruth-Ann, Ella was here before I could hang up the phone!" she laughed again. Mom kept assuring me that she was fine and I was not to worry about her at all. After talking for a little while longer, I spoke with Aunt Ella, told her I was on my way, but asked her to please not mention that to Mom, as she would worry about my being on the road and I didn't want to cause her any undue stress at this terrible time.

I worked out child care arrangements, told Alvin what happened and was on the road within the hour. Careful not to drive too crazy, I was able to make it to her side before dinner. When Mom saw me, she fell into my arms, crying inconsolably. She looked suddenly very old and frail, as if the storms of life had stripped her tree of all its foliage. I was so glad I had trusted my instincts and traveled to see her that day. She needed me. And I needed to care for her for a change. That night I slept in the house that Mom had fled from so early that morning. Mom begged me not to stay there, but I declared it to be the safest house in the city. No one would dare enter those doors after a shooting incident! I felt as if I could have slept in the house with the doors wide open and all the lights on inside and been perfectly safe. But it would be my final night in my childhood home. Mom never stayed another night there, and it would be years before she ever felt truly safe anywhere again. Perhaps she never did.

The man who broke into our home was a neighbor; he had cut grass and shoveled snow for my parents. It's still unclear what he was looking for that night, and I shudder at the thought of what was on his mind. But the bullet from Mom's .38 caliber gun entered his head about a quarter-inch below his left eye. A few centimeters in any direction would have killed him. He will bear the scars and residual effects of his actions for the rest of his life.

Months later in court Mom had to face him and relive that horrible night again before a jury of her peers. She was given the chance to speak before his sentencing and was quite nervous about it. When she asked me what she should say, and I told her, "Tell the Court you want three things: A bigger gun, a well-lit room and a second chance!" Although I consider that one of my better comebacks, she was mortified at the thought that she would ever consider taking a life. And truthfully, I was ever so thankful she did not kill him.

The perpetrator was given seven straight years for breaking and entering our family domicile early that late summer morning. I think Mom wanted him to get the electric chair, and I suppose that was a bit extreme. When he got out of prison, Mom was more terrified than ever, fearing that he would still retaliate. She relocated to Pittsburgh for a few years before eventually moving back to Saginaw to spend out the remainder of her days. I always regretted that this trauma happened to her so late in her life. Those scars seemed to never heal.

CHAPTER TWELVE

Letter From Okemos

When Tim and I found out that Jai was autistic, one of the first things Tim had encouraged me to do was to try to find my biological family. It didn't take much investigation to locate Child and Family Services of Michigan in the city of Okemos. After a few phone calls, I spoke with a woman who promised to mail the specific forms for me to complete and return. These forms would be on file should anyone from my family desire to find me. I requested non-identifying information, but I had to be specific about who could search for me. I remember well what I hand-wrote on the form as to who could contact me: Mother, Father, Sister, Brother, Aunt, Uncle, Cousin, Neighbor, Family Dog, Family Cat and Family Bird. My hope was that any reader of these forms would understand how open I was to anyone who might have been interested in finding me. I'd hoped the response would be immediate, or at least within about two to three months. With the passing of time, I had given up hope of ever finding out any information or family history. The request letter was mailed in the summer of 1984, a few months before our car accident. Further, with all that happened, I had just about forgotten I had initiated the request and it scarcely crossed my mind again.

On January 22, 1993, when Alvin and I had been married for about three years, a curious letter arrived at our home. The return address was from Child and Family Services of Michigan, Inc., , and it read like this:

Ruth-Ann J. Thompson

Dear Ruth-Ann,

In response to your request for identifying information in 1984, we are notifying you at this time that your birth sibling has contacted our agency. She has placed a consent on file. This form authorizes our agency to release her name and location to you.

Your sister's name is Janice [DOB]. She was in the 3rd grade at the time of your birth. Janice was described as an excellent student, having great leadership qualities. She enjoyed reading, took piano lessons and attended church and Sunday school.

We have your signed release on file. If you would like to have contact with this sibling, please call our office...

I couldn't respond fast enough and called the moment I finished reading the letter. I did my best to reassure the kind-sounding voice on the other end of the phone receiver I was VERY interested in connecting with my sister. She convinced me she would let Janice know immediately; however, it would be a few more days before another letter would arrive at my home from Child and Family Services of Michigan, Inc. dated January 23, 1993 –

Dear Ruth-Ann,

We are responding to your request for identifying information in 1984. As you know, we have recently had contact from your biological sister. She filed a statement of consent with our office, consequently, we are now authorized to release her name and location to you.

She is: Janice Welsh [address and phone number included] Additionally, I've enclosed non-identifying information regarding your birth family and a list of support groups.

Some people find it helpful to talk about their thoughts and feelings as they are making decisions about re-connecting with their biological relatives. If it would be helpful to you to discuss any issues you may have regarding your birth, adoption or the above information, please telephone me.

This letter included loads of non-identifying information, but reading it gave me a sense of belonging like I had never known before:

You were born 8/2/60 at St. Joseph Mercy Hospital, at the University of Michigan Medical Center, in Ann Arbor, Michigan. At birth you weighed 6 lbs. 6 ½ oz. and arrived at 7:07 pm.

There were no known medical concerns on either side of your birth family. Both of your birth parents were of African American descent.

The status of termination was voluntary. After much consideration, your birth mother felt that adoption planning would be in your best interest. She wanted you to have a loving and stable home.

Your birth mother followed the Baptist faith.

Your birth father had no known religious affiliation.

The document offered other non-identifying information about my biological mother and father, and my siblings. I discovered that my birth mother enjoyed reading and music, especially the piano. She had graduated from high school and planned to obtain additional training. My birth father had reddish-brown hair, medium brown eyes, and a reddish-yellow complexion, which described me to a "T". He was considered a steady and dependable worker with good health habits and was always neat in his appearance. He loved outdoor sports, especially baseball. In fact, he had belonged to a baseball team and was an excellent player. He had served in the military on two separate tours of duty.

It seemed that my parents had known each other since high school.

The letter closed with these words: *Your adoption was confirmed 9/18/64 by the Saginaw County Probate Court.*

I appreciated the other pamphlets included in the letter. There was an Adoption Book Catalog (Fall-Winter 1992-1993) with more than 100 book titles on various aspects of how to deal with the emotions surrounding an adoption. There was "Reunion Tips for Triad Members" – a triad consists of the adopted child, the parent who surrendered their child and the parent who adopted the child. And there was a list of Michigan Adoption Support

Groups and their contact information. To date I have never really read all of that, but I still value the fact that resources were made available at that time.

At approximately 4:00 pm on Thursday, January 28, 1993, my telephone rang.

"Hello?" I answered. Remember, this was before cell phones – most people barely had caller ID at the time.

A throat was cleared as the female's voice responded, "Hello. This is Janice Welsh…"

Uh-oh! My mind went into overdrive, forgetting the letter that had just arrived the previous day. Was this a bill collector? A telemarketer? A wrong number? Before thoughts got away from me, I heard her voice say, "… the adoption agency …"

And that's when the screaming commenced! I realized that I was speaking to my sister! My very own, flesh-and-blood, honest-to-God sister! I was breathless, sweating, freezing cold and experiencing a racing heart all at the same time as my happy voice quivered. "Janice? You're my sister?"

"Yes!" she responded delightfully. I could hardly believe what I was hearing. She began talking with me about my family, remembering when I was born and telling me that I had a bunch of siblings. She named them in birth order and told me where everyone was living and what they were doing. There were eight children on our mother's side, and two more on our deceased father's side, and I was right in the middle. With one conversation, I shifted from an only child to right in the middle of a large family! We spoke effortlessly, as if we had known each other our entire lives. Instantly I wanted to meet her face to face and I began to think of how we could connect with each other; there were so many speaking engagements I had scheduled over the next few months.

"I don't know when I can meet you," I said regretfully.

"Oh," she quickly responded. "I'll be there tomorrow. And I'll have our mother with me."

"That's perfect! Let me give you our address and basic directions." Again, remember this was before you could just enter the information into Google Maps. When we hung up from each other, I was tearful, excited and hopeful.

And suddenly I began to panic. Really panic! I cannot recall ever feeling as vulnerable and frightened in my entire life. I was filled with "What if's." What if it was all a scam and she wasn't really my sister? That would mean that I had given my personal information, address and extra details to a perfect stranger! What if she smoked? I did not permit any smoking in my house and if I told her she couldn't smoke; would she leave me alone forever? What if she wanted to take advantage of me; to rob me and hurt or even murder me? What if she met me and then rejected me?

I finally calmed myself by taking slow, deep breaths and then began to fret over every little detail. We had plenty of space at our home, so I wasn't concerned about where everyone would sleep. We had plenty of food, so I wasn't worried about feeding them. But how do you prepare meals for someone you've never met? What would we talk about for an entire weekend? How would my sons accept "Aunt Janice" and another grandmother? How would I properly explain all of this to them?

Over the next 24 hours, I sang, prayed, smiled, worried, prepared and did what I could to keep my composure, including doing a few celebratory dances! I even decided to color my hair a perfect Miss Clairol Chestnut Brown. However, the chemical concoction turned my hair maroon! I looked like a plum. I was so disappointed! Certainly, she would think of me as a complete failure and would laugh at me when she saw that my hair was the color of a freshly peeled beet! Oh well. What was done was done.

About two hours before their scheduled arrival time, I raced out of the house for one last thing. I recalled a familiar song entitled "Tie A Yellow Ribbon," sung by the group Tony Orlando and Dawn. The lyrics tell a story about a man coming home and feeling unsure if his true love still wanted to be with him. As he was riding on the bus, he recalled what he had written in his letter. He told his true love to "tie a yellow ribbon 'round the old oak tree. It's been three long years; do you still want me?" He declares that if there aren't yellow ribbons on the tree, he will just remain on the bus and forget about their relationship. As the song goes, when he arrived at his destination, the entire bus erupted in cheers, because there are a hundred yellow ribbons 'round the old oak tree.

So, I went to the fabric store and got enough spools to tie a hundred yellow ribbons around the old crabapple tree that grew in our front yard. I wanted Janice to know that she was welcome, and that I wanted her in my life. A neighbor, Kris, saw me outside and asked what I was doing. When I explained to her that I was meeting my sister for the first time, she helped me tie all those ribbons. I don't think I could have done it without her!

About twenty minutes after we completed that task, I was standing at the kitchen sink when I looked out of my window to see myself walking toward me. I couldn't believe how much she looked like me! And her hair was the perfect shade of beet maroon! I later discovered that she, too, had used Miss Clairol Chestnut Brown, which had turned her hair the same awful color it had turned mine! Oh, she looked so beautiful to me! When I flung open the door and hugged my sister, my heart felt at rest. She looked like me, talked like me, had mannerisms like mine. But she was the best part of me. Fiercely intelligent, deeply insightful, determined to succeed, loving and wise. I just don't have enough adjectives to describe what a wonderful woman Janice Welsh is. Little did I know on that day that she would become one of my dearest friends. I thank God often for the gift of my "Big Sis." And, by the way, she does not smoke.

Janice came with my biological mother, aka Bio Mom. Meeting her was anticlimactic for me. She was low-key, often insulting and, at times, downright rude. Soon after we met she coldly told me, "I didn't want you then and I don't want you now." She also told me, "I can't believe you still have that ugly name. I gave you the ugliest name I could think of because I figured someone would change it once you were adopted." Those words cut me deeply and it has taken me years to process and ultimately get over them. I have come to love my name, which is plain, simple and easy to read and spell. I have come to accept that I was born for a purpose and fulfilling it is my desire.

I understand now that when Bio Mom made the decision to surrender me for adoption, she had settled in her mind that she would never see me again. She had to find a place for me in her mind and heart, just to be able to carry on with her life. Her act of surrendering me was certainly the best thing she could have ever done on my behalf. She gave me a good start in life; I was born full term and healthy and was given an opportunity to live in a home far better than the one she could provide for me. Many times, I have wondered if my acceptance of these facts has simply given Bio Mom a "pass" just to be able to deal with it all. And perhaps initially that would have been true. But time and space have given me insights and clarity. Her choice gave me a fighting chance to survive and thrive in this world. Over time, I have come to accept and ultimately love her for who she is. It has taken many years and lots of personal work, but I am grateful to have this settled in my own mind.

Clarity came in an unexpected and perfect way in the early 2000's during one of my morning devotional Bible readings. I found a verse that caused me to ponder for months.

> On the day that you were born your cord was not cut,
> nor were you washed with water to make you clean,
> nor were you rubbed with salt or wrapped in cloths.
> No one looked on you with pity or had compassion enough to do
> any of these things for you.
> Rather, you were thrown out into the open field,
> for on the day you were born you were despised.
> Then I passed by and saw you kicking about in your blood,
> and as you lay there in your blood I said to you, "Live!"
> Then I passed by and saw you kicking about in your blood,
> and as you lay there in your blood I said to you, "Live!"

EZEKIEL 16: 4-6 (NIV)

I could relate to these words completely. On the day I was born, my Bio Mom didn't want me. She had her reasons, and I have learned to respect them; however, it doesn't change the facts. Finding her left me feeling tossed aside and it hurt me deeply. But God passed by and saw me dancing in that orphanage in Ann Arbor, Michigan. And even though I was a ward of the State of Michigan, God said to me, "Live!" Prayerfully I contemplated this passage. It was through this soul-searching process that "The Open Fielders" was born. The Open Fielders is my children's book series, written to touch the heart of a child and encourage the hearts of parents. Out of pain, God brought forth purpose and direction. He's good like that.

The weekend meeting with Big Sis and Bio Mom was a whirlwind. Friday night we went to our church for choir rehearsal and I introduced them to my church family. On Sabbath, we were invited down to the front of the church and our pastoral staff offered a beautiful blessing and prayers of thanksgiving over our newly-formed family. By Saturday evening my brother, Andre' and his young family had joined us from Cleveland and my sister, Tressa and her family came in from the DC area. We had invited the church family to join us, and they came bearing gifts of food and love – we had over a hundred people in our house that evening! Talk about a celebration!

My children were simply giddy. Jai, who normally didn't take change well, seemed to know that he was with family. He accepted them without incident. Brandon, always the quiet thinker, was spending time with everyone, listening and observing. Later he would tell me things about my personality and theirs that were spot on. Austin, only four years old at the time, kept getting me and Janice mixed up. It was frightening for him and he kept asking me if I could ever adopt. I always told him, without hesitation, that I could, indeed, adopt.

"You mean you could really adopt a child?" he asked incredulously.

"Why, yes, Austin! Certainly, I could. In a heartbeat! Without hesitation," was always my prompt reply.

It would be twenty years before I understood what he meant by that question. Without knowing it, I was confirming his deepest fears that he, too, could one day be "adopted" – or given away. When he was asking if I could ever adopt, what he was really asking was could I ever give one of my children away, offering them up for adoption. He spent twenty years of his life expecting to be given away. While finding my biological family granted me the answers I so deeply desired, it raised multiple questions for him that he struggled with for two decades. It's a reminder that you can be ever so loving, yet your children can still have questions and uncertainties. How I hate the fact that my youngest son felt vulnerable and potentially unwanted for most of his life! My misunderstanding of his simple question to me caused him to feel this way. We must be careful to speak life into our children and to confirm their questions, making sure we understand not just the words but their understanding of those words. Every choice we make, everything we say has a profound impact on those we love.

On that Sunday morning of our introductory weekend, we were visited by Linda Wilson Fuoco, a reporter from the Pittsburgh Post-Gazette newspaper. She came with Bill Wade, her camera man, and wrote a beautiful article about our reunion. Here are some excerpts:

Yellow ribbons festoon the mailbox, tree and porch lights in front of a yellow brick Penn Hills home. The ribbons welcome the long-lost relatives that Ruth-Ann Mosby met for the first time last weekend... the ribbons beckoned [Bio Mom] into the arms of the daughter she had never held or hugged. Though she raised eight children, she had never stopped thinking about the little girl she gave up for adoption 32 years ago. "I was an only child and I always wanted a brother or a sister," Mosby said yesterday. "Now I have eight. Be careful what you pray for," she jokingly told a reporter, as she introduced her birth mother, a brother and two sisters.

"We were very poor," [Bio Mom] explained. "I had five children I could barely feed, and I was divorced. It was not a popular decision in those days, but while I was pregnant, I decided the baby deserved a better life.

"I was highly criticized, but when I saw her in the hospital, she was just perfect. And I knew that giving her up was the best I could do for her. I never held her in the hospital, because I didn't want to bond with her. I knew if I held her I could never give her up. So, I didn't hold her until Friday."

Ms. Fuoco wrote a wonderful article that graced the front page of the Local section of the newspaper. She also mentioned my "real" mom in the article. Believe me, Mom had a lot of feelings to deal with as well. Versia Jones felt completely left out. In fact, she had asked me if she could come for the meeting, but I had told her not to come. Emotions were flying high and

I just didn't think I could handle anyone else's feelings but my own. It hurt Mom terribly to be told to stay at home, but I don't regret asking her to stay away. In time, she got the chance to meet all my siblings and the Bio Mom and they all loved her as much as I did. Eventually she saw my point of view, although she really did feel slighted that weekend.

The triad can be tricky. The woman who placed her child in adoptive care, the woman who adopted the child and the actual child, who could also be an adult by the time of meeting - each sees the situation through their own eyes and within their own reality. The choices to surrender a child are many and complex. The reasons for adopting a child usually involve pain, loss, struggle and multiple decisions. The child can fantasize about their birth parents and can assume they were somehow the reason for the adoption, feeling responsible for something that was never their decision at all. Each side may feel both benefits and guilt over the adoption. Meeting my family conjured up my core feelings of abandonment and rejection that I will continue to process for the rest of my life. Still, finding them has added a rich layer of love, slathered with respect. I am part of a great group of people who are spiritual, intelligent, hard-working and supportive. I've watched them face giants and conquer them, climb the mountain of education all the way to the top and demonstrate the necessary art of forgiveness. I've watched us love and lose with dignity and grace. I even discovered that I am related to a famous entertainer. Little did I know that the Letter from Okemos would be such a blessed gift.

There were so many things going on in my life during this season. Soon after finding my family, marital problems became too much to handle so I packed up and left Pittsburgh abruptly and painfully. The boys and I moved to Saginaw where I lived not only near my mom, but also very close to my biological family as well. It was wonderful to feel such unconditional love. With the loving support of Janice and her husband, Terry, I completed my court reporting degree and began working as a bona fide court reporter. What a sense of accomplishment for me. I stayed in Saginaw for three years, during which time my divorce was finalized. In 1996 we relocated to Charlotte, North Carolina where I not only worked as a court reporter but also caught the "classroom bug." I was given a wonderful opportunity to teach court reporting theory to the incoming freshmen. How I loved teaching! It gave me a great sense of pride to educate, encourage and enlighten the students of such a strenuous course. Court reporting success is all about consistent practice and I offered helpful tips that inspired them toward advancement.

A year later, much to the shock of everyone, including us probably, Alvin and I remarried and we all moved back to Pittsburgh and back to the same home I had fled four years earlier. My mother and Janice offered hesitant support, but I was living my life the way I chose. My church family welcomed me back with open arms, which made the transition much smoother. We decided to have a child, and one year later, almost to the day, May 1, 1998, I gave birth to my only daughter, Alexandra Janae. Mom, who was living in the city with us at that time, could not believe that she finally had a granddaughter, and the boys were in awe of their little sister. By now Jai was 16, Brandon 13, Austin almost 10. It was like starting all over again with parenting, but we had lots of support and Alex was an easy baby. She was the shining light of the household.

While Alex was still a babe in arms, I started a ministry, Beneath the B.A.R.K. (BTB) with Migdalia Brathwaite. This amazing ministry combined our love for trees with workshops, music, and presentations for children and adults. We spent long hours in prayerful preparation and used our own finances to fund this effort. We were invited to present all around the country in multiple venues. The time working on BTB was precious to me. We were both busy – I was teaching court reporting and Migdalia was completing her doctoral studies. Our friend, Allison, was taking classes as well, but still worked with us. Exhausting days and full weekends kept us all busy. Even my sons offered support and helped with research and development. Currently, Beneath the B.A.R.K. is on hold because we live in separate parts of the world, but I don't believe either of us have ever truly relinquished this provocative and life-changing joint vision.

I fell into bed one Friday evening, completely drained from the maddening pace of life. I expected to be sleep in no time, but the sound of music kept me awake. This music, beautiful and soothing, was playing so loudly that I simply could not rest. I got up to close my bedroom window, assuming the neighbors were outdoors entertaining. But even with the windows closed, the music continued. It would take a few minutes for me to realize that the song was playing inside my head. A lovely tune that I had never heard before.

Although still very sleepy, I realized what was happening. I got up, went downstairs, found a pen, some paper and a tape recorder, and sang the song into it. It was entitled C. J.'s LOVE SONG (You Are Mine). It's a song sung from God to man, stating that He formed us in the garden of His love, placed potential inside of us, will always be there to protect us. I love the words that God gave me that evening, confirming that He is the One who will always care for me.

> I am your Vine and your Provider
> I am the Fresh and Morning Dew
> I am your Trellis and your Arbor
> I'll always believe in you.
>
> I am your Sunshine in the shadows
> I am the Bright and Morning Star
> I am your Warmth when nights grow colder
> And I accept you as you are.
>
> I am the Lily of the Valley
> I am the One who calms the sea
> I am the fragrant Rose of Sharon
> You can always depend on Me.
>
> You are Mine … You are Mine … You are Mine.

This song ushered me into the incredible and unexpected world of song writing. Eight more songs came in rapid succession, usually when I was doing something else, like driving, for instance, or distracted in some other type of way. I simply cannot explain it. Various songs came to me and there was nothing that I do to assist the writing process. Before long I was recognized as a songwriter and was thrilled when songbird Christina Sinclair chose "My Savior and My Friend" to include in her "Praise from the Soul" CD in 2007.

To date I have released two CDs – "In the Garden" and "A Thin Place," each with its own purpose. Proceeds from the sale of "In the Garden" go to Two Scoops N-PAC, a non-profit organization that raises awareness for adoption, foster care, fatherhood and mental health. "A Thin Place" is dedicated to Brandon.

CHAPTER THIRTEEN

Teenage Mutant Ninja Turtles... Cowabunga!

Although we had missed Jai's initial appointment due to our accident, Tim's death and our injuries, I rescheduled his meeting for late spring of 1985. First, they discovered that he is not hearing impaired. Then came the other diagnostic testing. There were 16 signs that were used for screening and determining autism, and Jai displayed 7 of them. Now the popular buzzwords are "autism spectrum disorder" but at that time Jai was diagnosed as "Autistic-Like" which no one could ever truly explain to me. I knew there were delays and deficits, but what to do with that diagnosis left me puzzled. "What does autistic-like mean?" I asked one doctor. "Could I be considered Caucasian-like? Or overweight-like? Or comical-like?" He never seemed to have an answer or any real guidance for me, but I knew that early intervention was the key to Jai's lifelong success. Thankfully, one doctor suggested that I contact the Childhood League Center to see if I could enroll Jai into an early intervention preschool.

When I called the Childhood League, the voice behind the receiver sounded kind, understanding and interested in my concerns. She gave me loads of information, took some of mine and explained that Jai could be placed on a waiting list if I wanted. Yes, I wanted that. He would be number 55. She insisted that calling back to check his status would not be a bother to her and told me to expect paperwork in the mail. When we ended the call, I was both encouraged and concerned and didn't know where else to look. I did the only thing I knew to do – pray and believe.

In less than a week, I got the call stating that Jai's position had changed from number 55 to number 1 and asked if I were interested in a tour. When I inquired about the cost of tuition, I was given that magical number – FREE! Before long, Jai was climbing onto the bus and heading off to school. His teacher,

Grace Volker, was a gift from God. She was patient, tender, skilled and someone in whom I could trust to teach my child. There were eight children in her class, and we parents became very close during those unsure years. Jai made lifelong friends in that class and we keep up with many of them to this day.

Each time Jai changed schools, it took time for him to readjust and it was important to me to always choose a place that believed in his ability to succeed. Wherever he attended, I fiercely monitored their treatment of my son. I can remember one time I wanted him to attend a school where the teacher had multiple degrees and an impeccable record for her work with autistic children. But when we met her, she was dismissive to Jai, told me he was lower functioning than the students in her classroom, and said he wasn't a good fit. The "professionals" wanted me to consent to let Jai go to this other school, but I had already visited and determined Jai would never attend there! They trained children in the same fashion that one would train a dolphin or a seal, throwing "goldfish" snack crackers at the children whenever they answered questions correctly. Yes. I said THROWING. Worse, the kids were instructed to catch the food in their mouth, without the use of their hands. I sat in that meeting and refused to sign off on that foolishness.

"Well, what will you do with your child?" the question was offered in a condescending tone from the terse-lipped education director.

"I will keep my child home until this district comes up with a satisfactory solution!" was my immediate reply. Long before "least restrictive environment" was the standard, there was "Mama Ruth-Ann's Standards," and I wasn't just putting my son somewhere because "they" said it was the right place.

After two weeks they found a classroom at Thomas Griffith Elementary School in Dublin, about 20 miles away from our home, with one teacher who had just graduated from college. She was assisted by one full-time aide, and taught one full-time student, Jai Timothy Williams! I will always be grateful to Ms. Paula Brown, now Mrs. Derifield, young, energetic and completely committed to my firstborn's educational success. Jai was her star pupil for two full weeks until the district realized they had other children who would benefit from this unique classroom setting.

To get him to that school, the district chose to transport him by cab. He was still young and did not speak conversationally. So Ms. Brown and I communicated with each other via a spiral notebook, unbeknownst to the cab driver. I soon discovered Jai was not getting to school until well after 10:00 a.m. each day. This was completely unacceptable! At that time, I was nine months pregnant with Austin, so I asked my friend, Lauretta, to drive with me to follow the cab, lest I would go into labor while conducting my investigation. We were shocked to find that this man was leaving my child in the car unattended while he went to breakfast, visited a lover and even out shopping! He knew that Jai and Bobby, the other child who had now joined the class, could not speak, therefore he falsely assumed that he could get away with that nonsense. Remember this was in the days before cell phones and Facebook, or I would have certainly exposed him. But I did contact the school district immediately, and never saw that cab driver again! Trust me, the replacement driver was also followed ... and proved to be a conscientious and caring transporter of children.

There were plenty of other times too that I chose the teacher's heart over experience. Once when we lived in Saginaw, this teacher, who looked like Henry Winkler's character, The Fonz, from television show Happy Days, walked into an introductory conference meeting sporting a black leather jacket, sunglasses and a slicked-back hair do. He declared, "Well, these kids can't learn a darn thing. Not a darn thing! And I promise you this: I'll be worse than some of his teachers, but better than most. But I tell ya right now, don't expect nothin' from your boy. He won't learn a darn thing."

"He sure won't," I quipped, "Not from you because he will NOT be in your class!" And I exited the meeting swiftly. That year, I chose to have Jai repeat the fifth grade, even though he didn't need to do so academically. It turned into one of the best years of his schooling, and I am so grateful that I did not subject Jai to that buffoon. He was fired before Christmas break.

Life passed far too quickly and before I knew it, I was attending Jai's high school graduation in June of 2001. Mom, Aunt Ella and Cousin Barbara came down from Saginaw, but we were only given four family tickets to attend the event. Alvin stayed home with Brandon, Austin and Alex, while we went with Jai to the packed auditorium. Words are inadequate to describe the pride in my heart. He had overcome his bleak prognosis, and it felt as if his entire life paraded in my memory that day. When Jai's name was called, over two-thirds of the graduates and all the faculty gave him a lengthy standing ovation. He walked across that stage, his gold honor cord swaying with each step, and confidently shook hands with the dignitaries of Penn Hills High School. It made my heart sing. This child of mine had endured so much, overcome so much and progressed in a way that I could have never imagined. I'm convinced that the other one-third of the class that didn't stand, simply didn't know who he was, or surely, they would have applauded as well.

After graduation, Jai attended classes at the local community college. One quarter proved to be a huge challenge for him, but I have always admired his willingness to try. He began working at KFC. Back then it was still called Kentucky Fried Chicken. He was there for over five years before another work opportunity was offered to him. Getting Jai to this point has taken years of trial and error, and a mother who aggressively monitored his educational process. He is a wonderful asset to the community in which he lives, works and worships. Always helpful, ever kind, his passion is photography and he expertly takes candid shots that look amazing. When he sees people he loves, he stands in front of them and combining American Sign Language with speech says, "Teenage Mutant Ninja Turtles ... Cowabunga!" We don't really know why he does that, but he has done so for years, and that's just who he is. People never seem to mind his greeting and respond with kindness and warmth. I believe that Jai is going to be okay, and I believe that's what his greeting means.

Brandon challenged my parenting skills in quite a different way than dealing with autism. Brandon was real active, very vocal, quite personable and extremely intelligent. I tried putting him in preschool, but it wasn't a good fit. He was far too advanced and became a nuisance to the students and teachers there. By Kindergarten, his teachers wanted to advance him to first grade, but I wanted him to be with kids his own age. I began to supplement his learning, giving him extra work once he got home from school. He didn't seem to mind at all and often finished those assignments much sooner than I anticipated.

He was blessed to have Karen Jones as his first and second-grade teacher in Pittsburgh. She taught in a multi-grade classroom, but knew how to challenge her students beyond what they ever thought possible. She told her students they could be anything they put their mind to, and even called them by their "professional names" to enhance their belief in themselves. Spiritual, active, a lover of math and science, Brandon thrived under her instruction. Throughout his academic life, she remained his favorite teacher.

We relocated to Saginaw by the time he was in the third grade, but within two weeks of starting school, he had lost his love of reading. Naturally concerned, I contacted his teacher, but she didn't seem to know, or care about my child or what was wrong. I inquired about his day and discovered he was completing all his assignments for the day by about 9:45 in the morning. When the children finished their work, they could – you guessed it – READ for the rest of the day! I asked her to give him extra work, even if she didn't grade it, just to give him more of a challenge, but she refused. I was quite disgusted with her dismissive attitude.

I decided to get him tested, and I called the Department of Education to get information. The whiny and annoying voice on the phone said, "Oh, Honey, every parent thinks their child is gifted. (scoff, scoff) If you want to get him tested, and find that he is just as average as everyone else, it will cost you $140."

"And if he is above average? What then?" I insisted. This woman had irritated me to no end!

"Well, then we cover the cost of testing and look at placement in a gifted program. But if I were you, I wouldn't ..."

"Thank you for your time," I interrupted and slammed down the receiver, and made the call to schedule him. They had an opening the very next day.

So, instead of going to that awful Read-a-Thon class at the private Christian school, I took Brandon to be tested. There were fancy words and graphs and charts presented, but basically, he scored in the high-genius range on the IQ testing. This was the ultimate proof that man doesn't know all, for my doctor didn't expect him to be "viable" before his birth. It gave me great joy to make two more phone calls: One to the teacher explaining that he was officially unenrolled from that classroom and the other to the whiny and annoying voice at the Department of Education. The teacher was suddenly interested, concerned about retention, and wanted to know if there was anything she could do to change my mind. Brandon, after all, was such a "wonderful addition" to her classroom. Child, please! I wasn't trying to hear that from her – not now! And Ms. Whiny-Voice had already received the information and had put in the request to pay the $140 to the testing branch of the Department of Education.

"I guess you were right about your son," she whined.

"I guess I was," came my smug reply.

Grades three through eight Brandon excelled in the various gifted programs he attended. He was one for whom learning came easy and could navigate those classes with ease. His teachers loved him. It was wonderful to see him smiling again.

For high school, he chose to attend a private boarding school, Pine Forge Academy, a co-educational high school nestled in the hills of rolling green on the River Manatawny, about 60 miles west of Philadelphia.

Unsure how to pay for this expensive venture, I prayed earnestly for God to open financial doors for Brandon. I was gratefully and unexpectedly promoted to the chairperson of the court reporting department of Duff's Business Institute. Running the department was pure joy for me, combining my appreciation for the craft, my organizational skills and my love for people. I worked well with the college president, my coworkers and the teachers in my own department. The $17,000 pay increase more than covered the cost of tuition that year. But after that year, just as suddenly and unexpectedly, the court reporting department closed, I lost my job and didn't know what we were going to do.

This period of my life strengthened my faith in God because I did not know where else to turn. We made it through these trying years. I worked part time as a court reporter for Allegheny County. Beneath the B.A.R.K. afforded some financial reward, but nothing steady. I worked temporary jobs as well, and yet somehow Brandon's tuition was paid. He worked each summer and part time during the school year. Anonymous donors contributed to his bill. I can recall his senior year when all moneys had to be paid before he could take his final exams or go on his class trip. I would not get paid until after that due date and didn't know what we were going to do. I did not want him to worry or be overly concerned about finances, but I was impressed to encourage Brandon to pray as well. I did what I could to encourage him, but I saw no way for this bill to be paid. Imagine my surprise when he called the morning of the testing day to tell me that his grades were so high, he had exempted out of all his finals! That gave me time to get the tuition paid before graduation.

I was one proud mother of one of the graduates of the Magnanimous Class of 2003. Alvin and I and his three siblings were excited to witness this auspicious occasion. Brandon graduated third in his class. He was offered multiple awards and scholarships and had a bright future ahead of him.

He was granted full rides to multiple colleges, for both his bachelors and master's degrees; but Brandon chose a different path. His love for engineering and music drew him to Full Sail University in Winter Park, Florida, just outside of Orlando. Because there were no scholarships to this prestigious school, Brandon worked and saved money, determined to fully fund his college experience. A hard worker and determined saver, he relocated to Florida the next year and started a journey of his own. The program was rigorous and sometimes he would call so discouraged, but after listening to him and offering words of encouragement, he sounded like he could make it. He became a man down there in Florida and I found him to be compassionate, caring and nurturing. His home became a shelter for many a weary traveler and he was quick to share from what little he had. I was extremely proud of him!

When graduation time rolled around, I didn't have the money to attend his graduation. I was devastated! Two days before we were to come, I decided to call and prepare him for the fact that we might not be able to make it. He seemed somewhat distracted with our conversation, and then quickly said, "Mom, I'm gonna call you back." I hung up thinking, "Did he not hear what I told him?" Within minutes, he called and said, "Hi Mom, do you have a pencil? Write this number down." When I asked why, he said, "Just do it."

I called the number and heard a thick southern drawl. "Hello? I'm Brandon Williams' mom ..." "Yes, Ms. Williams. I understand you need to get to Brandon's graduation. I'm looking at flights now, and there's one for $473, that will put you here by ..." As the conversation continued, I made a request: For less than that amount of money I could drive my car and all of Brandon's siblings could be there too. "Fine," said the voice. "I'll wire the money."

Not wanting to sound ungrateful, I simply HAD to know who my benefactor was! "Well," said the voice. "I'm not wealthy, but I'm well-to-do. Brandon has tutored me consistently and has never charged me one thin dime, even though he knew I was a man of means. I am convinced I owe my degree to Brandon. And if his mama needs to get to the graduation, his mama's gonna get to the graduation!"

We packed quickly, picked up the wire-transferred money, got on the road and headed to Florida. Staying with friends in Charlotte, we made it a two-day journey and arrived on a Thursday afternoon in early February 2007. Arrangements had also been made for us to stay at the Embassy Suites, which included a full-service breakfast. Brandon's church family provided meals for Friday after the graduation and Sabbath after church. The only uncovered meal during our stay was paid for by the hotel. We travelled there and back without incident and witnessed Brandon earn his Associate's Degree in Recording Engineering from Full Sail University. He was again the third in his class, and celebrated by his mother and siblings. And while there, I got to meet our generous benefactor, Roland.

True to his nature, Austin's educational career was filled with adventure. It is said that "hindsight is 20/20," meaning that one can always look back and see where different choices would have been better. When it was time for him to start Kindergarten, he had begged me to stay home, and I really should have given him a little more time there, especially since his birthday is in September. But I pushed him out of the nest way before he was ready to fly. He struggled in school. Designed more for the practical world, the classroom was a place of boredom and near torture for my third son. He made friends easily, everyone liked him, and yet he was the constant jokester, getting into trouble for every little thing. I was deeply concerned that my child seemed to hate learning and I wanted him to have opportunities in life that I believed only a proper education would afford him. And I certainly didn't want him labeled as a trouble maker.

By the time he was in third grade, I was brought in for a conference and told Austin had attention deficit disorder and needed to be placed on medication. I was furious. I don't know if it was the years of dealing with autism and giftedness, but I just felt that I could not deal with another "issue". When we got home that day, I pulled Austin aside and yelled in his face, "We aren't gonna have any of this! You are going to school, you're gonna pay attention and I don't want to have another meeting about your behavior. You don't have A-D-D ... you have B-A-D ... and I will spank your A-S-S if you don't stop it right now!" He stared at me as if I had sprouted ten heads, then said, "Mom, I think you said a bad word somewhere in there." I knew in an instant that my reaction was the wrong one.

We eventually tried medication, but for only a short time. The pills caused him to lose his appetite, his eye looked glassy and as he explained to me, "Mom, I feel like I'm running really fast inside, but my feet aren't going anywhere." The doctor kept saying that we needed to give the medicine time to work, but I stopped it within the week. I didn't like the drugged-up version of my active son. We tried dietary changes, such as less sugar and a little meat, more veggies and extra water, which helped a lot. We made sure he got plenty of exercise, which also helped. I've always said that Austin would have benefited from having to walk three miles to and from school every day. I even tried to home school Austin for a while, but ultimately expelled my own child from home school!

When Austin was 12, I began to fear that he was heading down a dangerous path. Multiple school suspensions, failing grades and questionable choices could no longer be ignored. After much research, I chose to take him to a place called "Miracle Meadows," nestled in the remote mountains of West Virginia. My grandfather would have said that the location was "behind God's back" which was his way of saying "in the middle of nowhere." This was a school for at-risk youth and he didn't know in advance that he was going there. We all piled into the car and drove the two hours down and over to Salem. Once there, the dean took Austin to one area while the director talked to Alvin and me about what we could expect. We were to have no contact with Austin for two weeks and were cautioned that when we saw him again, he would be very angry with us and not want to have much interaction with us at all. It was a teary ride home for me! Had I done the right thing? I really didn't know.

I dreaded the next time I'd see him for fear that my child would be angry with me, but we dutifully arrived on schedule two weeks later. When Austin saw us, he let out a loud hoot akin to a country farmer and came bolting across the fields to meet us. Full of smiles, he gave bear hugs all around and began to excitedly tell us what had been going on during his time at Miracle Meadows. "Mom! You see this ditch here?" He was pointing to a ditch that looked to be miles long and several feet deep. "I dug this ditch! Did most of it by myself!" he proudly explained. "And you should see the size of the RATS I killed near the kitchen! Bigger than CATS, Mom! And do you know I can tell the time of day with my arms?" Then he extended his arms and began to move in a robot-type fashion to imitate the hands on a clock. His face displayed a huge smile and he was talking a mile a minute.

Our time together was wonderful, very different from what had been predicted. Seeing Austin there gave me hope. More importantly, he'd met wonderful teachers, mentors and counselors from all over the world who have still remained a part of his life. Although that place is now permanently closed, I am grateful it was there when our family needed somewhere to land. Austin was at Miracle Meadows for nine months while Brandon was at Pine Forge Academy. The costs for both places was astronomical and I know it was only God who helped us pay those bills during that time in our lives.

By high school, my youngest son was attending an alternative high school which fit his style and personality. He had teachers who cared and was given educational options that insured his success. It was a blessing to witness him march across the stage to receive his high school diploma. Brandon now lived in Florida and was unable to attend the celebration, but we planned a surprise 18th birthday party for Austin in September of that year and Mom, Brandon and his mentors from Miracle Meadows, along with my friends from Columbus, all came into town to support him. I'm so grateful that event was recorded and I have watched the DVD many times since. Those were precious memories.

Austin has become a great man. He's a fantastic father to sons Elijah and Jaidon, and an entrepreneur with multiple successful business ventures. How fitting that he is a comedian and entertainer. Although we live miles apart, we are closely connected. He still brings a smile to my face whenever we talk or spend time together.

Eventually the second marriage to Alvin ended in divorce too. This time around we agreed to co-parent Alex and remain friends despite our differences. Together, with the help of God and loving support of family and friends, we managed to raise a phenomenal daughter whom we both love dearly. Our divorce took its toll on her, however, as anyone would imagine, and yet I do believe she appreciates two parents who get along well and provide her with the freedom to love them unconditionally.

I had resolved I would never remarry. The pain of loss was too great and the work required of marriage was nothing I was willing to do. Songs, speaking engagements and writing assignments, in addition to work responsibilities and church duties filled my life quite completely.

So, it was a pleasant surprise to get a call from Kirk Thompson, a pastor friend from my Oakwood days. Kirk and I had shared great times at the student center interacting and playing games, laughing and kidding with each other. And he was the lead vocal in a premier quartet, Step Up to Happiness. How I always loved to hear him sing! He now lived not far from Pine Forge Academy and pastored in Philadelphia. Our conversations were filled with depth and I never seemed to want to hang up when we talked. We finally began to spend time together and met each other's children and extended families.

I couldn't wait for him to meet Mom. While visiting her in Saginaw, Michigan, he got down on one knee and proposed to me in front of her. I couldn't believe I was getting married again! We began making plans, but decided to dispense with all the fanfare and have a simple ceremony in the Prayer Garden at Allegheny East Conference campgrounds, the campus of Pine Forge Academy. We married on 07/07/07 at 7:07 am. I surprised him by singing a song I wrote entitled, "Completely Answered Prayer." There wasn't a dry eye among our intimate group of supportive friends. Jai was the only one of our children in attendance. I have always regretted that all our children weren't there to bear witness to our love. My marriage to Kirk was a blessing and we were the greatest supporters of each other's dreams. Kirk recorded a CD, "I'm Still Here" in 2012, pairing more of my original songs with his phenomenally smooth-sounding tenor voice. Our home was happy, filled with love, and a welcoming beacon to countless others.

December 13th of 2007, Elijah Jason was born, and Austin, my youngest son, became a father. This beautiful baby was one of the cutest I had ever seen and our family fell in love with him. After a time, we moved to Columbus, Ohio and settled into life there.

In September of 2009, Aunt Ella called to tell me Mom had a stroke. I tried to calm myself as I drove up to Saginaw to be by her side and was amazed to find she was still able to talk, walk, move and nothing seemed wrong. But her doctor pulled me aside to offer grim news. Although she seemed fine, she was about to embark upon a series of mini-strokes, and one of them would surely take her life. "Keep her comfortable, help her adjust to her new limitations; we have done all that we medically can do for her."

Mom and I would spend much time together over the next three months and her last days were peaceful ones. She had visitors and neighbors, family and friends surrounding her day and night. About 2:00 am on December 19, 2009, exhaustion swept over me like a rushing current, as I whispered to her, "Good night, Mom. I love you. I'll see you in the morning." The nurses came in an hour later to tell me she was gone. I did not lose the color in my world when Mom died. Perhaps it is because her death was not a shock to my system; Mom had lived a full life and had prepared for death. Still, I have no words to describe the empty, aching pain I felt in my heart. Utter loneliness and sheer gloom engulfed me and consumed my soul. My champion, my strength, my hero, my mother! I fell beside her bed and thanked God for giving me such a wonderful mother. It was my privilege to be raised by such a woman. I remained until the funeral home came to carry her body away. The tall gentleman was very tender when he suggested I step out of the room as they prepared my mother's remains. But it was my privilege to stand stoically by and watched him gather sheets, tuck her away and carry her out in a body bag. I left that facility and went to Denny's. It was just before 6:00 in the morning. The perky waitress greeted me kindly and escorted me to in a corner booth. After ordering my meal, I called my dear friend Allison and began to cry...

My family knows how to come together in times of crisis. Their love and support surrounded me and buoyed me up. We buried Mom on the 23rd, and returned home that same day. It was as if we could hear Versia Jones demanding us to "Visine our eyes," and we determined to make Christmas a joyful celebration. I am so grateful to my children, as well as Jennifer (Elijah and Jaidon's mother) and Maria, Brandon's girlfiend, for caring for me during this time.

2010 brought more losses and precious gains. Uncle Don died early in the year and Aunt Kathy died just a few months later. I believe she died of a broken heart; the love of her life and her best friend died within months of each other and it must have been awful to bear. It was my privilege to spend a few nights with Aunt Kathy that April. We laughed and talked for hours about old times, life and love. And then she was gone by autumn. Then August 15, I had the joy and privilege to witness the birth of Jaidon Emanuel, born in Pittsburgh. As I watched Austin holding that newborn son in his arms, I was amazed at how mature he had become. My "baby boy" holding his baby boy was a healing balm for my soul. And Elijah was so excited to have a baby brother!

If I sit long enough, memories of my parents return to me and I always smile through my tears. The stories they told, the interactions we had, the laughter we shared fill my heart with love, peace and joy.

CHAPTER FOURTEEN

Thank You Everyone For Coming!

When Brandon was a little boy, he was quite active and rambunctious. No matter how much we practiced "quiet time" at home, he just could not sit still in church. Well, let me back up a bit. First, he hated dressing in fancy suits, ties and shoes. Many are the days he would be completely undressed by the time we pulled into the church's parking lot. Several Sabbaths, Brandon would have thrown a shoe or his tie out of the moving car while en route to worship services. Finally, I began to drive to church with Brandon still in his pajamas, having packed his church clothes to dress him once we arrived. So just getting him dressed "properly" was always a challenge. Time and wisdom have taught me I should have simplified his dress, appropriate yet non-suited-vested-buttoned-tied-up with shoes that were shiny but hurt his feet tremendously.

But once we arrived at church, Brandon was convinced that everyone in the entire sanctuary was there just to see him! He would burst through the doors, extend both arms heavenward and declare in his outside voice, "Thank you, Everyone, for coming!" Try as I might, I could not persuade him the congregants were not his personal guests for the day.

He enjoyed wearing bright colors and fiercely loved the pastors of our church. He wanted to go up to the front, sit on the rostrum or at least sit on the deacon's laps who, at that time, sat facing the congregation week after week. There were youth programs and Pathfinders, and Brandon was a part of it all. Pathfinders is a worldwide co-ed youth organization like Boy/Girl Scouts. He sang in the youth choirs, even having solos from time to time. Once before I spoke during divine worship, Brandon sang a beautiful song, and toward the end of his rendition, he got tickled and then laughed through the entire final chorus.

As he grew, he changed into a quiet and reserved young man, his friends' confidante and his siblings' champion. While at Full Sail, he met Maria through a mutual friend, Teri. Maria lived in Missouri, and we met her when she joined Brandon for Tim's mother's funeral in South Carolina in 2007. Maria was a quiet, soft-spoken, beautiful dark-haired beauty, of mixed Pakistani and Caucasian descent.

Over time Brandon relocated from Florida to Missouri and thankfully, after my mom died, Brandon returned to Columbus in 2010. He worked faithfully for almost two years at a local gas station. A regular customer noticed something special in Brandon and offered him a "real" job at a company called Forward Air. He earned a substantial raise, great benefits and a work schedule that allowed him to pursue his passion of musical engineering. He was finally in his sweet spot.

Not every June 16th is Father's Day, but 2013 would be the fourth time in Brandon's life Father's Day fell on his birthday. On that morning, he, Maria and Alex were all in the kitchen with me as I prepared our traditional Sunday morning "Big Breakfast." When I told him "Happy Birthday," instead of saying, "Thank you," he asked me when I was going to get him his Father's Day present. Puzzled, I responded, "When you become a father." To which he asked the same question again, "So, when are you going to get me my Father's Day present?" I was getting a bit annoyed, but Alex immediately started jumping up and down with excitement and squealing with delight. It took me a minute to realize that this was his way of announcing that he was going to be a father and I was about to be a grandmother again. I was thrilled! Maria said she was feeling well, and all was right with the world. They had decided to move to Valdosta, Georgia, which is where the baby would be born and they would begin their lives together as a family. Soon after his birthday, Maria moved down there to get settled while Brandon remained in Columbus to negotiate his transfer.

He had been working on a project at his job and had shared the particulars with Alex. He was convinced that completing this assignment would reap substantial professional benefits for him. The night of July 31, 2013, he and Alex along with Jasmin, my grandsons' sister, stayed up late watching comedies. As I climbed the steps to bed that night, I could hear Brandon laughing a hearty, belly laugh. It caused me to pause on the stairs, turn around and look at him. He had such a beautiful smile. He looked happy and content. Alex and Jasmin were thoroughly enjoying themselves as well. My heart was filled with gratefulness.

The next morning was very busy. Thursday, August 1, 2013, Alex was scheduled to get her long-awaited-for braces. I had taken off work for the next two days. After getting her braces, we would head to Pittsburgh to spend time with Austin and the children. One of our stops would be to Kennywood, an amusement park that was sure to be a crowd pleaser. We would celebrate Jaidon's 3rd birthday a few days early, and since mine is August 2nd, I felt like I was celebrating mine as well. My birthday with my grands! What a gift it would be!

Kirk and I dropped Alex off for her braces. It would be about two hours or so, and we chatted like young romantics and thoroughly enjoyed our time together. When we arrived back at the dentist to pick up Alex, she went on out to the van while I went into the office to complete the final paperwork. Before I could finish, she ran back into the office, insisting, "Mom! We have to go! We have to go now!" A bit perturbed, I said, "Oh my goodness! I'll be there in a minute!"

As I headed to the driver's seat, she explained that Maria had called to tell us Brandon had been in an accident and was being Life-Flighted to Grant Medical Center. When I heard the words "Brandon" and "Accident" in the same sentence with "Life-Flight" my heart felt heavy and ice-cold. My thoughts ran rampant and washed over my mind like a torrential downpour. "I can't do this again, Lord!" I heard myself screaming to the heavens. "I can't do this again! I WON'T DO THIS AGAIN! I can't lose anyone else! And in a car accident? No! No! NO!" Kirk suggested he drive, but I had already pressed the accelerator, heading for the hospital. My mind was racing, yet my heart had stood completely still. I remember not being able to feel my legs or arms, while I tried to control my breathing, remain within the speed limits and get to Grant Hospital.

I had Alex call Maria and as I spoke with her, she shared with me every detail she knew. A coworker had connected with her on Facebook and told her Brandon's car had gotten hit right in front of his job. Talking with her helped to calm me down because I was trying to keep her calm and assured. She insisted that she was going to make the 10 hour drive up from Valdosta, and I wanted her to be rested and safe. She had to take care of my unborn grandchild; Brandon's unborn baby.

Somewhere between getting the news, talking with Maria and driving to the hospital, the Lord gave me a sense of peace and blessed assurance. I had made a pact with God on that 20-minute journey: "I'm gonna let You be God, and I'll be me. And whatever I have to go through, I'm gonna praise You and hold on to Your hand." Gratefulness would be my watchword. When we arrived at the hospital, I was told Brandon had been flown in by the Life Flight helicopter and he was in surgery. Determined to find gratitude in every situation, I whispered, "Praise God. They don't operate on a dead man. He's alive."

Within the hour our pastor, our conference youth director and a few of Brandon's co-workers arrived. The waiting room seemed sterile and boring, with uncomfortable seating and limited visiting hours, but it would be my home for the next six days. There was no way I was leaving that hospital when my child was there. Initial reports said a man ran the red light, hit a semi-truck and then hit Brandon. "Praise God," I declared. "Brandon didn't take a direct hit."

When Brandon was out of surgery, they let me and a coworker go back to see him, even though it was not during the actual visiting hours. "I'm here, Brandon," I said with as much encouragement and reassurance as I could muster. "You are not alone. I love you." With that, he extended his right thumb upward and gave me two fist pumps. That gesture would be his final "thumbs up". By that evening, Maria had arrived. The next day my sister, Janice and her daughter, Tina, from Lansing and my girlfriend, Allison from Pittsburgh arrived. My friends in the medical field, Robyn, Anita and Elethia, were helpful in explaining in laymen's terms what the doctors were saying. Linda, who had been there with me as my coach when I gave birth to Brandon, was checking on us constantly. Many others, too numerous to name, were there to give comfort and support and I don't have enough thank you's in my heart to express how much their calls, texts, visits and prayers meant to our family during that trying time.

All were attentive to Maria as well, making sure she ate and drank, even when she didn't feel like doing so, and they were caring for Alex and Jai as well. Kirk, who had been diagnosed with End Stage Renal Failure, had dialysis treatments on Mondays, Wednesdays and Fridays, so he was there when he could be as well as helping to keep things together at home. By Saturday, Austin arrived from Pittsburgh and many other family and friends came from far and near. Most, including Austin, stayed for the weekend. Many promised to keep in contact and to return whenever we needed them. On Monday, Tim's siblings, Brandon's Aunt Barbara and Uncle Ron, came in from South Carolina.

We settled into a rhythm at the hospital. The staff gave us access to the workout room so we could shower. We were given discounts on food from the cafeteria. We all slept in the waiting room, carefully managing our time with Brandon. The church elders and deacons, members and friends poured into the hospital, most bearing gifts of food or games; all offering prayers, love and support. We had plenty to share and other families, gathered in the waiting room for their loved ones, enjoyed the blessings of our food, prayers and encouragement. It's so wonderful to be part of the family of God.

Our updated accident report confirmed that Brandon had been hit first by the speeding, 60-miles-per-hour, red-light-running driver. My child had taken the full brunt of the impact of that cargo van on the driver's side door of the black 1994 Honda Prelude that he had driven and worked on for years. His car was then spun out of the way into the median as the driver, Norman Cooper, also slammed into an 18-wheeler semi-truck causing damage to its radiator. The doctors kept telling us that my son was "very sick" but I was just so grateful that he was alive. "Praise God," I insisted, "that in spite of taking such a hit, he is still with us." I was determined to be grateful.

Brandon had a total of four surgeries to attempt to repair his broken body. At the time, we were told that he had a broken femur, spinal injuries, and multiple severe internal injuries. It would be later that I discovered the extent of those injuries. The trauma surgeons had initially operated to stop internal bleeding. His incision was kept open and his swollen intestines were covered with saran-wrap-type covering. Once when I was in his room, I asked the nurse if I could see his abdomen. "You won't want to see that," she said matter-of-factly. But I insisted. And when she showed me, I did not flinch or shutter. This was my child and my prayer was that God would heal him completely, from the inside out. Over those precious six days we had many quiet moments, just the two of us. I spent time just looking at Brandon, the features of his face, the detail in his strong body, the curves of his hands, the shape of his toes. It reminded me of how I had looked at him when he was newborn, tracing every detail with my eyes and etching every marking in my heart. That time – a treasured memory. I took that time to declare my unwavering love for him, to pray over him, to sing him lullabies, to talk to him.

Whenever people would come to see Brandon in Room 309 of the Intensive Care Unit at Grant Medical Center, they would usually pray over him. Before they left, we would see tears escaping his shut eyes and rolling slowly down his cheeks. "Praise God, he hears every expression of love and every prayer," I'd whisper to myself.

Alex had been at the hospital with me and Maria during this entire ordeal. On the night of August 5th, I decided she should go home with our cousins, Kevin and Patty. They understood what we were facing, since they had lost their son, Johnathan, the year before. I felt she would be in good hands and needed to lie down and get some "good" rest. She didn't want to leave, but I was insistent. Maria and I would remain at the hospital. We said our good-byes to Alex and settled into our little corner of the waiting room. Suddenly, Linda returned to visit us! We were so happy to see her! She said that she decided to return and just spend the night with us. Linda was like a breath of fresh air for us, always full of laughter and love. She has tons of funny stories and humorous anecdotes. She was just what we needed to lift our spirits and bring us hope and cheer. Her visit was another reason to praise God. The three of us were like teen-agers in that hospital that night! We ran up to the cafeteria at midnight to eat French fries and burgers! We pushed all the buttons on the elevator and laughed about silly stuff well into the night. Finally, sleep overtook us about 1:00 am. My last thoughts before dozing off were happy ones.

About 2:00 am we were awakened by the hospital staff. We could hear "Code Blue" alerts over the intercom. The nurse told us that Brandon's heart had stopped beating. Without waiting to hear what else was being said, my blood ran cold and I raced to the bathroom. All I could hear was them calling "Code Blue" over the hospital's intercom system. I couldn't breathe. I couldn't see. I couldn't feel. My world turned black and white. I exited the restroom and found Linda's loving arms awaiting me with a smile on her face. "They revived him! He's gonna be all right!" she exclaimed. I exhaled loudly and fell upon her shoulders sobbing in relief, color returning to my sight.

No sooner had I walked back into the waiting room and sat down when the doctor came out and asked me to follow him into a small room. "I'm not going in that room!" I cried! "I'm not going in that room! When families are called into that room, the news is not good!" Maria's beautiful brown eyes looked bewildered and petrified. Linda was looking at me in disbelief. I knew I had to go into the room, but I certainly didn't want to. I took a deep breath and slowly entered the room, refusing to sit down. My entire body felt as if it were made of lead.

"Brandon is very sick," the doctor began.

"Sick?" I queried. "What does 'sick' mean? When I hear 'sick' I think it means like having the flu or a bad cold. What does 'sick' mean?"

The doctor inhaled before continuing. "He needs another surgery. I am not sure why his heart stopped, and we need to find out why, but he is too weak to take back to the operating room. We will need to do the surgery at the bedside."

"Can we see him?" someone asked. I don't know if it was me, Maria or Linda. This entire memory is one huge horrible nightmare.

We could go back and see him, but just for a minute. We clutched each other as if our very lives depended upon it. I would surely have fallen over had they not been there. "Praise God that Linda decided to stay," was my heart's grateful prayer.

Within the hour the doctor called us back into that dreadful room and told us there was nothing more they could do. Brandon's intestines were dead and blah-blah-blah. Whatever else he said, I failed to hear. He patiently and methodically explained what was happening to my son – necrotic bowel, extensive internal injuries, failing heart - but all I could hear was distorted phrases and confusion. He could have just as easily been reciting one of the lost languages. I stared at him, unable to make out the features of his face. I finally inhaled deeply and asked, "Do we need to call in the family?" "Yes," was his solemn reply.

At 4:30 am Kirk answered on the first ring. "Please wake up Jai and go pick up Alex and come to the hospital right away. Brandon has taken a turn for the worse. It doesn't look good." At 4:32 am Kevin also answered on the first ring. "Good morning, Kevin. I'm sorry to wake you. Brandon has taken a turn for the worse. Kirk is on his way to pick up Alex."

"We'll be praying," Kevin's tender voice broke as I pressed the disconnect button on my cell phone. I called Austin and left a heartbreaking message. I didn't want to leave too much information, but he needed to know what was happening. He later told me he knew when the phone rang ... I tried to reach Barbara and Ron, since they were in town from South Carolina, but I couldn't remember what hotel they were in and didn't have their cell numbers. I couldn't seem to do much of anything. My head was spinning as I tried to think of anyone I had forgotten or overlooked. My mind simply could not think properly at such a time as this.

There were no visitation rules enforced as the family began to arrive. We gathered around Brandon's bedside as he lay so still, and said our goodbyes. First, I sang the lullaby I used to sing to him as a child. It was written by John Denver and is entitled: For Baby (For Bobby). I chose this song because of the phrase, "I will love you more than anybody can." And I sang as if my very life depended on it. I was determined to give Brandon the sweetest of memories during his dying breaths. When I finished the loving lullaby, the doctors and nurses were standing around and there wasn't a dry eye in the ICU, including tears exiting Brandon's eyes. My heart was broken and I had no way of knowing what to do with it. Yes, he was 28 years old, about to be a father. But he was my child! My baby! I had nothing to give to anyone else. All my attention and love was focused on Brandon. His final hours would be filled with all the love we could give.

We played all kinds of music, for Brandon loved every genre. We laughed about happier times, recounted family memories and assured him repeatedly of our love for him. Then we began to see his numbers drop – blood pressure and respirations. The last number I remember seeing was 50/32 before we were hurriedly ushered out of the room. The last time I saw him alive, someone had jumped onto his bed, straddled him and was aggressively administering CPR while doctors flooded his room. We again heard the Code Blue call over the hospital's intercom system and I knew, again, that they were referring to my second born son.

About 8:10 am that same doctor emerged from those huge oak doors to tell me that my son, Brandon Je'Zhon Williams, had died. He didn't say a word. He just looked at me through tear-stained eyes. I simply asked, "What time?" He replied, "8:05." Maria almost collapsed. Alex was inconsolable. Jai stared into oblivion. Kirk looked frozen in time. I felt as if my body had disconnected from my mind. It felt as if I could feel my lungs trying to find air and I felt the blood flow stop in my body. My lips were moving and sound was escaping, but I have no idea what I was saying, or if there were words at all. The feeling is impossible to describe. The pain is impossible to explain. The world is impossible to understand. I could see absolutely no color anywhere I looked. At that instant, all the color drained out of my world. It would be about three days before the color would begin to return, but to this date, it has never been as vibrant as I remembered it once to be.

We were able to go back in the room with him. No more tubes. No more breathing apparatus. No more IVs. Just us and Brandon. He looked like he was sleeping. Like he would just roll over and jump off that table and say some deep and profound statement about life. He didn't look dead. He didn't look gone. He didn't look like a part of me had been amputated never to be attached again on this earth. By now people had heard and had come. The room was once again filled with members offering prayers and love and support. Brandon said it best all those years ago, "Thank you, Everyone, for coming."

Eventually we had to leave. I was once again alone with Brandon for the last time. And it was then that I realized that we were in the very same room I had been given 29 years earlier when my own husband had died in a car accident.

ICU Room 309 of Grant Hospital. In 1984, I laid in that room and prayed that my unborn child would survive. In 2013, I stood in that room beside my lifeless son's body. "Praise God," I offered in determined and resolute worship, "that I was the vessel through which Brandon entered this world. The Lord giveth and the Lord taketh away. Blessed be the name of the Lord."

Alex, Maria and I went into Brandon's room that night, huddled together and clinging to one another with all the hope that was within us. On his message board, he had written these words:

> Every day when I wake up,
> I tell myself it will be my last.
> If you are not trying to hold on to time,
> You are not so afraid of losing it.

I believe this statement is from the book *Gregor the Overlander*, a novel written by Suzanne Collins. But that time, it was a message that resonated deeply with us. As we all gathered to say goodbye, I happened upon a pamphlet on grief. It offered that people die three times in life – first is when the breath leaves their body and physical death occurs. Second is when the person is funeralized or memorialized. But the third death is the last time anyone ever speaks their name. As long as I am alive, I will always speak his name. I was suddenly grateful that Mom had not lived to see me lose Brandon. I don't think she could have survived it all.

There was another wrinkle to the depth of grief I experienced. The man who hit Brandon was not ticketed for his offense. He should have received a traffic violation for Failure to Obey a Traffic Control Device or Failure to Control, or something. But in Jackson County no one saw the need to "inconvenience" this man with a traffic citation. No one tested his alcohol levels or anything. I was in constant contact with the sheriff's office and the officer on the scene, but no one seemed worried about Norman Cooper's inability to stop at a red light. Witness reports confirmed his actions, but the justice system was slow to act. In November of that same year, he died of a massive heart attack. I felt sad. His family was now also thrown into the deep end of the pool of grief and loss.

We were elated that Maria chose to stay with us during her pregnancy. She had an easy time, and we were all extremely joyful and grateful to focus on a baby. Many were the days that I would look at her and know what she must have been feeling. Seeing her was a painful reminder of the time I carried Brandon after becoming a young widow. Carrying a child during indescribable grief and sorrow is a tall order for any woman to fill, but Maria did it with grace and determination. It was my joy to be her birthing coach, and along with her mother, Barb, we witnessed our granddaughter's entrance into this world on Valentine's Day, 2014. Shandon Ja'Naan is the perfect combination of her parents, and we are thrilled to have a portion of Brandon with us.

The days and months after Brandon's death I felt numb. Numb and nameless, as if I no longer knew how to identify myself. I had been born an orphan and lived in an orphanage for the first four years of my life. Everyone knew what an orphan was. And I had been widowed when my first husband was suddenly killed in an automobile accident. I was a widow for almost six years before remarrying. Everyone knew what a widow was.

But now I had lost a child and I had no name to identify this experience. There was no word that could be used to describe who I had now become. And worse yet, I would be this nameless being for the remainder of my life and beyond, really. The woman who buried a child.

Online searches produced a word, "vilomah" from an article written by a Duke Professor of English, Karla F.C. Holloway. She explains the word like this: This idea of orderliness and the disorder of a child's death eventually brought me back to the Sanskrit word "widow." And as creative as I thought I might be with language, as liberal as I was willing to be in borrowing a word from another language -- maybe from Swahili or Greek, French or Thai -- or even creating one myself from a collection of letters that I might shape into the meaning I needed, I returned to the language that had already given us one word. I considered that Sanskrit might locate another. And I found "vilomah."

Vilomah means "against a natural order." As in, the grey-haired should not bury those with black hair. Our children should not precede us in death.

If they do, we are vilomahed. Her explanation fits, to a point, but I personally have never accepted that I was a "vilomah."

I went to the Bible and I found where Naomi referred to herself as "Bitter" after having lost two sons along with her husband. (Ruth 1:20-21) But I chose to not become bitter, so this name doesn't fit me either.

It would be a few years before I would choose the name "achromatic" for myself. I was "achromatized" when my son died from injuries sustained in an automobile versus cargo van deliberate. I call it a "deliberate" and not an "accident". When Tim and I were hit on October 14, 1984, that was truly an accident. All traffic was stopped on the interstate and the driver had no way of knowing or anticipating that to be so. He tried to miss us, choosing to veer to the left and partially into the concrete divider to avoid hitting us. That's why Tim received the brunt of the force and why Jai's car seat was pushed into my ribs. It was an accident. But I call Brandon's a "deliberate." A man was exceeding the speed limit by more than 20 miles per hour, plowed through a red light and hit my son directly in the driver's door. The car's door was pushed all the way over to the gear shaft, with my child pinned between. The fact that Brandon survived at all is a testament to how good and faithful God is.

And yet the pain of losing a child is unbearable at best. As I'm writing these memories, I'm reminded of a Facebook post I wrote on November 7, 2015: "Another family I know lost a son this week. They too were members of 'the three boys' club' and then also had a daughter. Our children grew up together. Attended Pathfinders together. Performed together. Enjoyed camp meetings and youth federations together. My heart goes out to them. And to all grieving parents. Grieving parents don't stop grieving until the day they stop living. Grieving parents are unnamable. Not orphans. Nor widows. Yet still just as empty and heartbroken. It took a while, but I think I have found my name. I now consider myself achromatic."

Achromatic is relating to, employing or denoting lenses that transmit light without separating it into constituent colors. It literally means "without color." And that's the best way I can try to describe my feelings. Most days I feel like I'm achromatic. Like I'm standing at the window peering into a sea of vibrant fall foliage and rich, colorful skies, but the color has been somehow removed from view. Like if sound had colors, I'd be severely hearing impaired. Like if vision had hues, I'd be almost totally blind. Like if motion had pigment, I'd be a quadriplegic. Like if music had shade, my feet could not find the rhythm. Like life goes on and passes through me, all around me, and yet I simply am unable to comprehend it fully. Like the movie is playing on the big screen; just without any color at all. Call me Achromacia. Achromacia-Ann.

The accident that occurred the day before my 53rd birthday should have killed him instantly, and yet Brandon continued to survive and exist for six days. Six days were gifted for us to shower on him all the love and care that we have. Visitors from around the city and family from across the country rushed to his bedside. They stayed and prayed and held his hand. They rubbed his head, sang tender songs and quoted meaningful salvific scriptures from the Holy Bible. And when they left, they always stated these life-giving words, "I love you, Brandon." Each time those words were spoken, we saw tears slowly exit the corners of his eyes. Alex recently told me that hearing is pure and unadulterated. Our eyes, sense of taste, smell and touch can deceive us. But whatever comes into our hearing is untouched and pure. During those six days Brandon laid in ICU, he could hear our love for him. Our words, promises, prayers and songs affirmed him and assured him of how deeply he was loved and how much he mattered to each one of us. All that occurred in the six days before I became achromatic. And before my children became "sib-achromatized." That's my word for them; for they've also lost some of their ability to see true colors because their sibling has been taken from them.

I was convinced that I would never sing again. Still able to praise God for His mighty acts, I just didn't think that song writing and music would be gifted to me again. How could music ever be born again? How do you sing when your heart is broken? How do you minister to others in song when you yourself have no song to sing? I did not know the answer, nor did I see it materializing any time soon. And yet on September 6, 2014, while spending quality time with Austin, this haunting tune, complete with verse and song came to me:

Ruth-Ann J. Thompson

Been hit with a pain so deep,
I'm on my knees
My soul's been crushed
There's no other Place, no other Help I know
No way to begin to heal
This hurt I feel
So, Lord, I trust
You'll bring comfort to my grieving soul

Many the tears I've cried,
The pain inside
The night won't end
Please tell me how long until the dawn will break
Many the miles I've travelled,
Glad I've got my
Heav'nly Friend
To comfort me, for Goodness' sake

Seems like the music's stopped –
The rhythm's dropped
My feet can't dance
Seems like all the air has slowly left the room
Seems like all the color's gone –
No rainbows found
Please understand
Speak Light into this doubt and gloom

Lord, restore my heart! How great Thou art!
Your love's so rare!
I fall on the Rock, no other Help I know
And out of my darkest night,
You shine Your light
Now I declare
You bring comfort to my grieving soul!

It was such a blessing to be able to release my second CD, "A Thin Place – Where Heaven Touches Earth" in the spring of 2016. My angel and benefactor, Roland Trevino, who helped me get to Brandon's graduation all those years before, along with Tony and Karen Williams of RealBiz, mixed the music for us and another Full Sail friend, Lucas Willey, created the cover. This project is dedicated to the memory of Brandon and proceeds from its sale go to the Brandon Je'Zhon Williams' Scholarship Fund, to help children attend summer camp. Alex sings "My Grieving Soul" with me; her voice so pure and sweet and her emotion so full of truth.

My only daughter has been a joy and delight since the day of her birth. So very different from her brothers, she was quieter, more intuitive, self-motivated. Alex has always lived her life in her own unique way. She's not easily manipulated and has always had wisdom far beyond her years. Daddy Frank would have said she was born with "Mother Wit," which is a way of saying that she has good old-fashioned common sense.

In addition to her parents being older when she was born, multiple mentors poured into her. She spent lots of time with my mother, and with her brothers. Her godparents, Kevin and Janet Currie and Uncle Hubert and Aunt Gretchen Mosby are loving and supportive. My dear friend, Allison, and her beautiful daughters, Valynn and Nicole, were often around. Migdalia and her sister, VJ and many others have helped to shape her into the woman she has now become.

Of all my children, she is the one who attended the most schools. In elementary, she had one year of home school, one year at private school, and one year in on-line school. She attended Jessie R. Wagner, which we called "The Little School" in Pine Forge, Pennsylvania, when we lived there. Then we relocated to Columbus, Ohio and she attended Columbus Adventist Academy (CAA) off and on until 8th grade. With all this jostling around, I wanted her high school years to be steady and uneventful.

She chose to attend Mount Vernon Academy (MVA), a private, boarding SDA school that was an hour away from home. I expected her to be homesick, but her freshman year was great. She made lifelong friends, worked and joined the acrobatics team during that time. When she headed home for summer vacation, she was excited about her future. We all were.

But then the accident happened. The day after Brandon's funeral she went back to MVA. I should have considered how difficult this would be for her. I should have been able to anticipate that she needed to be near us and take time to heal. My intention was that she would be surrounded by her own support system and she could keep her life as "normal" as possible. But there is no such thing as normal life after losing the ones you love. Healing takes even more time than you calculate it should take.

How she struggled that school year! I got her into counseling up there at the school, but it wasn't enough. By the Christmas break, we knew she needed to come home permanently. Alex was dealing with such unspeakable grief! We all were, really, and trying to help each other cope was next to impossible. The second half of her sophomore year, she went to The Arts and College Preparatory Academy (ACPA) in the city. Just being at home was somewhat helpful for her emotional well-being, but it's rarely enough help when you feel as if you are drowning every day. I was steeped in grief, trying to work, and attempting to function and maintain. I had nothing to give to Alex or anyone else. My storage was empty.

Somehow, by sheer will and grit, Alex survived that school year and the next one at ACPA. She had started driving and was adjusting to her life. For her senior year, she decided to go to the school that was just around the corner from where we lived and to which she could drive. This was by far her worst year yet, and I began to pray specifically and daily for Alex, with my dear friend, Patty. Every day felt like we were in cold, muddy, waist-deep water, trudging uphill, in the rain, walking backwards, without shoes. Even the day of her graduation, we were apprehensive.

Alex chose a one-year course in Massage Therapy as her vocation. At the time of this writing she has completed that study, passed her Ohio State Boards and is a licensed Massage Therapist working in her field. She is also a Phlebotomist, and works in that field as well. She loves children. My only daughter is well loved and well respected among her colleagues, clients, and the families she works with. And you should see her dance! When she moves, music comes alive! I have full faith and confidence that the next generation will be just fine.

In the summer of 2016, Alex and I were driving from Columbus, Ohio to Huntsville, Alabama. I was amazed to see how many Forward Air trucks we noticed along the way. I lost count as we watched the countryside change from green plains to small hills filled with the deep brick-colored clay that is common in the South. Every time I see one of those trucks I am reminded of Brandon's brain child and how he figured out a way to get more trucks on the road, thereby increasing productivity for the company. Just like his father, whom he never knew, he had also finished that task the morning of his car accident. And both would be pleased that their projects were completed ahead of schedule. During that trip, this prayer came to my mind:

> Now I wake me up to work
> I pray my duties I'll not shirk.
> If I should die before the night
> I pray the Lord my work's all right.

Yes, Tim and Brandon. Your earthly work was all right. I pray that you are both resting in peace.

I buried Brandon two rows away from his father in Greenlawn Cemetery in Columbus. On Resurrection Morning, as Tim is being called from his dusty grave, he will be able to look over his left shoulder and see his son for the first time. More importantly, Brandon, will probably see Tim first, recognize something very familiar about him, and I can hear his quiet, resolute voice asking, "Dad? Is that you?" as they both rise to meet the Lord in the air. And so shall we ever be with the Lord. No more sorrow. No more pain. No more separations. No more accidents or "deliberates." This belief brings a bit of color back into my world. At least for a time...

A few months after Brandon's death, I began to have difficulties with my health. My blood pressure was creeping higher and higher and would not stabilize. I generally did not feel well most of the time. A family doctor confirmed a diagnosis of hypertension and gave me medication to take, but I refused to use it. Kirk was naturally concerned and finally offered an ultimatum: see another doctor or take the medicine. So, I found a naturopathic specialist who gave me a thorough exam. I was in with her for two hours. It was there that she told me I was suffering from something called "takotsubo cardiomyopathy" which simply means that my heart was broken. Many people have heard of people dying of a broken heart – well that's a real diagnosis! That knowledge began the long process of seeking to heal my heart physically, emotionally and spiritually. A long and lengthy process indeed.

Next, I began to lose pigmentation in my skin. "You have vitiligo," the petite dermatologist informed me. "We call it the 'Michael Jackson Disease.'" When I told her that I was a part of his family, she didn't believe me. Truthfully, when I found my family, I discovered that Joe Jackson and my biological father are first cousins. And no, I've never met them.

My doctor's face looked sincere as she shared this with me, "We rarely see the manifestation of this in someone over the age of 40. You must be under a tremendous amount of stress or have suffered severe trauma in your life." Trauma indeed, Ms. Skin Doctor, I thought to myself. Trauma indeed.

Amazing how fancy names are given to life's challenges. Slowly I'm losing the pigmentation in my skin, my hands are spotted, my legs are displaying patches of non-color, my lips are no longer the beautiful shade that never required lipstick. It doesn't change who I am on the inside, but my outsides look like they've been through a war. Not only can I not see color when I'm in major crisis, now my skin is losing color as well. This lets me know that this pain will last for the rest of my life.

Overall, though, I really thought I was doing well. I was in counseling and talking through my problems. I was beginning to do the things that I loved to do. And I really felt as if my grieving was something manageable. But by the summer of 2017, I found myself often sad, and mostly very tired, exhausted and drained.

While sitting at my desk at 1:00 pm on September 27, 2017, I began to feel pain, ever so slightly, in my chest. It didn't really feel like my chest – more like the area above the rim of the left strap of my bra. It wasn't too much, and wasn't too awful, but just nagging and stinging – almost like a paper cut that had gotten alcohol in it. By 1:30, I mentioned to my supervisor that I wasn't feeling too good, but didn't feel that the squad needed to be called. I just wanted someone else to know what I was feeling. By the time I got home from work, the pain had intensified and around 6:00 I told Kirk that I felt I needed to go to the emergency room. But first I called my "doctor" – my dear friend, Robyn, who is a cardiac nurse. No answer, but I left a non-alarming message. Then I called Marc, our families have been close for years, and after describing my symptoms, his tone changed from jovial to serious. I needed to be seen at the emergency room.

I first went to the wrong location, an Urgent Care facility that was ill equipped to handle chest pain of any kind. So, I drove to a "real" hospital. Robyn met me there. I'm still amazed that it took almost 24 hours for them to diagnose a life-threatening situation. All the other testing showed no cause for alarm, but the cardiologist finally decided I needed a heart catherization, to be performed by Dr. Cardwell.

The procedure was explained to me in laymen's terms, which I really appreciate. There would be a thin long tubing, called a catheter, inserted in an artery in my right arm and threaded through my blood vessels directly into my heart. Aside from the insertion point, I was assured there would be no pain and the procedure would take approximately 15 minutes.

I was wheeled into the room and found myself laughing and joking around with the technicians and doctors, offering comical quips and jokes, singing along with the music playing in the room – THAT OLD MUSIC AIN'T GOT THE SAME SOUL ... I LIKE THAT OLD TIME ROCK AND ROLL!!! – using my outstretched arm as my pretend guitar.

Dr. Cardwell explained the process as he went along. "All right," he said, "I'm in your heart now. Let's take a look around."

"You hit my heart faster than Cupid!" I joked and laughter erupted in the room.

Suddenly everyone got very quiet, and Dr. Cardwell asked, "Has anyone in your family ever dropped dead of a heart attack?"

"No," was my solemn reply. And I hope no one's dropping dead today, I thought.

"Is there heart disease in your family?"

"Not that I know of." My throat went dry. I knew this was a life-changing moment.

That's when my cardiologist explained to me that I had a 95% blockage in the left anterior descending (LAD) artery, which he told me supplied blood to about 85% of my heart. "We are going to fix it by putting a stent in your artery. You are going to be fine, but you are a very lucky woman," he said matter-of-factly. The painless procedure did not take long, but without it, I'm told that I would have either gone to sleep and never awakened or dropped dead while walking along one day. This particular blockage is nicknamed, "The Widow Maker" and as I am finding out now, most people don't survive to tell what symptoms they were having before this type of attack. As the doctors were intent on performing their life-saving techniques, my silent, streaming, grateful tears were dropping onto the lab's table.

My broken heart, repaired by skilled physicians, is still in the healing process. But this I do know: my life has been preserved for a God-ordained reason. I vow to spend the rest of whatever time I have left on this earth to be the best representation of His love and grace to everyone I meet.

Life in all its forms is precious.

CHAPTER FIFTEEN

Gathering All My Belongings

In the spring of 2011, Kirk's kidneys failed him. The doctors told us that he might not survive this ordeal. Privately I was told he had three months or less to live. I asked the team not to tell him that, for fear he might give up. But when I went back into his room, it was obvious he was afraid.

"They say I might die ..." tears welled up in his eyes.

"Oh, you're gonna die," I responded, "but not today."

My emphatic tone made him smile and he began the long three-month journey to recovery. After three weeks in the hospital, he spent another two and a half months in a rehabilitation facility to build his strength and adjust to the grueling seven-hour dialysis treatments offered three days a week. We celebrated each milestone. Initially the process of thoroughly filtering and cleaning his blood helped him to feel better. He soon returned to driving, and sought to return to the pulpit, but he was unable to carry on his pastoral duties any longer and was placed on medical disability.

That was a challenging transition for him and yet I watched him continue to minister to others. Even though he couldn't preach, he would still visit his members on non-dialysis days. Eventually we relocated to Ohio where he finally completed his only solo project, "I'm Still Here," comprised of 10 songs I wrote, a hymn and the title song written by his lifelong friend, Deborah Hardy. To have his voice digitized was a blessing indeed.

He began a prayer ministry of calling to pray with others over the phone. Social media became his platform to connect, engage and advise. Someone would cross his mind, and he would call, email or message them to encourage and uplift. Even though he had earned a master's degree of divinity in his early 20's, he was open to biblical discussions with anyone and made God's Word simple and uncomplicated. How I loved to study the Bible with him! He also diligently connected with other pastors, many of whom had been in the seminary with him, and offered a confidential, experienced and listening ear sprinkled with tons of positivity. Kirk even used his various dialysis centers as a different kind of pulpit to spread God's message of love, grace and salvation. Together we rejoiced when his treatment time was lowered to only six hours, which is still a long time. He wanted so desperately to have kidney function again.

Our home was filled with all types of music and he could often be heard singing loudly at any given time. His voice remained strong throughout his illness and he sang whenever, however and wherever he could. He was given the part of Caiaphas the high priest in an Easter cantata, More Than Just a Man, and really bonded with the cast members. Even in failing health, he still commanded the stage and audiences loved his performances. I admired how he just kept moving forward. When he couldn't stand to preach, he sat. When he could no longer deliver sermons, he wrote. When that became difficult, he called or texted or prayed. When he could no longer attend church, he watched online and offered constructive feedback to the speakers. His final trip was to Pine Forge, Pennsylvania where it was his honor to dedicate his grandson, Tristan, to the Lord.

Kirk was well known as the lead second tenor voice in the Step Up to Happiness Quartet. Their rich voices and tight harmony were the perfect blend to bring delight to the hearer of their songs. David Chandler sang baritone, Thaddeus Jackson was first tenor and Stephen Richardson held the deep bass foundation. These four were more like brothers, having known each other since high school, and it was understood they would always keep in touch. Thad became desperately ill, and Dave and Steve planned to visit him in Florida, but Kirk was unable to join them. That's when I realized how sick my husband really was. Had there been any way he was able to get there, he would have. When Thad succumbed in 2017, Kirk was devastated. On the morning of Thad's funeral, Kirk arose early, got fully dressed, sat up in a chair (which was difficult for him to do) and watched his dear quartet brother's services online. He was inconsolable. For days after I would catch him wiping tears and hear him listening to quartet music.

January 2018 Kirk turned 60 years old. His sister, Kim, sent signs for the yard – a dozen black and white cows with the words, "Holy Cow! Look who's 60!!!!" on them. When he drove out of the garage heading to dialysis he saw all the grazing cows on the lawn and called me immediately just like I knew he would. His laugh was hearty and full.

Since he could no longer go out to dinner and his strength waned as the day wore on, I planned a surprise brunch at our home. I called him down for breakfast one Sunday morning, and there stood his dear friends, Robert, Janice and Crystal, along with their families. There were also local family members and friends in attendance as well.

Eventually Kirk's life consisted of dialysis and the bed. He left only to go for his now five-hour treatments and returned to our room. His steps were very slow; he used a walker to move around and his breathing was labored and heavy. I marveled at my husband's positivity and humor in the face of great physical challenge. He didn't complain or whine. He remained kind and caring. And I felt the end was near. I began to pray a three-fold request: 1. That he wouldn't pass out while driving. (In fact, we were discussing the need for him to secure transportation and I considered taking time off work to transport him.) 2. That he wouldn't collapse while home by himself. And 3. That he wouldn't die alone.

God answered all three prayers. During his dialysis, Kirk slipped into unconsciousness. He was transported to the hospital and it was again my pleasure to be by his side. During our time together, I assured him of my love for him, promised him that I would be all right and talked about the things that meant the most to us as a couple. Well wishers and members came to visit and his lifelong friends, Donna, Daphne and her daughter Danielle, along with Steve and his wife (and my dear friend) Margie made the journey to see him, encourage him and sing to him. After five days in surgical ICU, we knew he didn't have long to live. Via the phone his children and siblings told him how much they loved him, and one of his mentors in ministry, Elder Henry "Butch" Fordham spoke words of comfort and peace to him. A young man, Cole, from Oakwood University sang to him as he was passing, thanks to Alex's request, and the last song Kirk heard was, "The blood that gives me strength from day to day – it will never lose its power." Although in a semi-conscious state, he tried to open his eyes upon hearing our voices. His heart rate slowed steadily, and he passed peacefully with family, pastors and friends by his bedside. This gentle giant with a heart of pure gold closed his eyes in death on October 18, 2018. I miss him terribly.

Whenever we stayed at someone's house or in a hotel or anyplace that wasn't ours, Mom would tell me, "Gather all your belongings before we leave." It was vital that I looked around, under every bed, behind every door, in every nook and cranny for anything that might belong to me. Many times I would look, declare that I had everything, only to have Mom come behind me and retrieve plenty of overlooked items. I simply couldn't believe I had missed all those things! As I got older, I learned that it's routine for a mother to find all the belongings; and it's an acquired skill. But make no mistake about it, I do not leave things behind any more.

As I am living now on the "back side of 40" I know how important it is to gather my "belongings", my children and my grandchildren and let them know that they have someone in their corner who loves them unconditionally and prays for them daily. It is imperative that they understand that they are part of something greater and are destined and equipped to make the most of their time here on earth.

There was a reason why the first words I whispered to my children and my grandchildren on the days of their births were, "You belong to me. I love you." That feeling of belonging is so vital to my life and I want them to always know they are not alone. I have not done everything right. There have been plenty of times when my children, I'm sure, have felt alone. But I pray that they have always known that they are wanted, loved and that they belong.

Forever my four children, and anyone they love, belong to me. I lovingly gather all my belongings – those who belong to me, to share this story of my life. My days are happiest when there are gatherings at my home, around my kitchen table. We laugh, share and love on each other with a fierceness that has no limits or boundaries.

During labor, just before his birth, the doctor informed me that Brandon was in the occiput posterior (OP) position. Basically, he was trying to enter this world face up, and his skull was in the front of my pelvis. Labor was painful, but when the doctor rotated him minutes before his birth, the process of turning him was excruciatingly painful, made even worse considering my broken and not-yet-healed ribs. But the process had to take place for him to arrive in this world safe and sound. During his passing, Brandon's accident turned my world upside down, and considering my breaking heart, and the fact that his father died in the selfsame way, his death was made even more agonizing.

It was my privilege to stand at the dying bedsides of Mama Anna, Daddy, Mom, Brandon and Kirk. There are simply no words in any language to describe the depth of my anguish. But watching them in their final days on earth has prepared me for my own death. Whenever it shall come, I will not fear it. Brandon has gone before me, and I will rest with him and all who have passed from this earth. I know that my children will be able to handle my death, for their resilience and strength have shone forth through tears, during insurmountable challenges and indescribable grief. They amaze me every day. They have proven that they know how to carry on, to smile through their loss. They will know how to make something good out of the ashes of heartache and yes, they will rise as the proverbial phoenix. I pray that they will continue to love those who belong to them ... and that this cycle and circle of love gets wider with each passing generation.

I am, indeed, as happy as a field lark in plowed ground. This was my grandfather, Daddy Frank's saying. As a farmer and tiller of soil, he watched the larks descend upon the plowing fields as he turned over the dirt to reveal the earthworms below. "Planting season is the happiest time for a field lark," he would muse. "I do all the work and they get all the worms!" He would flash his toothless grin as his eyes twinkled, and I felt loved and secure. In all the challenges that have come into my life, I know this for sure: in my season of planting, God has done all the work, and I have gotten all the worms – the sustenance that has made me joyful, happy and free.

I declare that in my life, I've been through great loss and excruciating pain; endured unspeakable grief and profound sadness. But I have also known pure love, wild passion, multiple gain and deep fulfillment. And I now resolve that God can plow all the dirt he wants to; just let me enjoy His fresh air and sunshine. Just let me continue to bask in the rays of His warmth and love. Just let me continue this journey and trust that wherever it leads me, He is there to sustain me.

Dance has been inside me since the conception of all that is me. I started out dancing in a colorless, gloomy existence with no real hope or opportunity. Throughout my lifetime I have chosen to dance in the face of adversity, heartbreak and challenge. And I believe that one day I will dance in the sunlight of God's love for all eternity. Whether times are great or whether times are awful, whether I live for 50 more years or 50 more days, my daily choice is to dance, to smile and to celebrate. Despite everything, my journey is filled with joy.

> Though the fig tree does not bud
> and there are no grapes on the vines,
> though the olive crop fails
> and the fields produce no food,
> though there are no sheep in the pen
> and no cattle in the stalls,
> yet I will rejoice in the Lord,
> I will be joyful in God my Savior.
>
> The Sovereign Lord is my strength;
> he makes my feet like the feet of a deer,
> he enables me to tread on the heights.

HABAKKUK 3: 17-19

CONNECT WITH AUTHOR

Contact me: www.RuthAnnThompson.com

Follow me on Twitter and Instagram: @RuthAnnThomps

Like my page on Facebook: www.Facebook.com/RuthAnnThomps

Write me:

Ruth-Ann Thompson, LLC.

P.O. BOX 30221

Gahanna, OH 43230